MAR -- 2006

The Secret Life of Water

Also by Masaru Emoto

The True Power of Water
The Hidden Messages in Water
Messages from Water, volumes I–III

The Secret Life of Water

Masaru Emoto

Translated by
David A. Thayne

ATRIA BOOKS
New York London Toronto Sydney

BEYOND
WORDS
Publishing
I   N   C

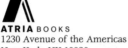
ATRIA BOOKS
1230 Avenue of the Americas
New York, NY 10020

Beyond Words Publishing, Inc.
20827 N.W. Cornell Road, Suite 500
Hillsboro, Oregon 97124-9808
503-531-8700   www.beyondword.com

Editor: Julie Steigerwaldt
Managing editor: Sarabeth Blakey
Copyeditor/proofreader: Marvin Moore
Design: Jerry Soga
Cover design: Carol Sibley
Composition: William H. Brunson Typography Services

ISBN-13:   978-0-7432-8982-5
ISBN-10:   0-7432-8982-X

Library of Congress Control Number: 2005931916

First Atria Books hardcover edition October 2005

10 9 8 7 6 5 4 3 2 1

ATRIA BOOKS is a trademark of Simon & Schuster, Inc.

Printed in Korea

For information regarding special discounts for bulk purchases,
please contact Simon & Schuster Special Sales at 1-800-456-6798
or business@simonandschuster.com.

The corporate mission of Beyond Words Publishing, Inc.:
  Inspire to Integrity

The universe, silence, a world stretching into
all eternity

> They came here from far away—hundreds and thousands of clumps of ice—moving through outer space. After a long journey through the expanse between planets and stars, the grand journey is about to come to an end.

The earth, emerald-green, shining brightly

> As the ice approaches earth, it enters the atmosphere and begins to break up, gradually becoming smaller, spreading out, and then finally falling to the ground.

Clouds, ornaments in the sky, art evolving moment
by moment

> When the ice granules fall to a certain point, they become a fine curtain of mist and spread out in the sky, creating a white carpet above the earth. A cloud is born.

Rain, ice granules falling down on plants, gently providing moisture

> Rain falls, bringing nourishment to the earth— forests, fields, flowers. The water sinks into the ground only to emerge ages later as springwater.

River, splashing, sparkling, flowing magnificently

> At first a muddy stream, the water eventually becomes a river flowing through the meadows—waterways, carrying life within.

Sandy beach, blue sky, sparkling ocean reflecting the sun, white waves

> Aeons ago, this is where it all began. The ocean gave birth to life and life emerged on land, creating a new day—the birth of bustling culture.

Morning mist, droplets flowing down the veins of green leaves

> Water, in its most pure and beautiful form, rises up in the cool air of the forest morning, creating a mist.

Beside the water well, nice and cool, the laughing
of children

> The children share a watermelon. Plants take
> their moisture from the ground, providing us
> with sweet fruit. Water from the well is cold and
> delicious.

Industry, chimneys, black smoke, discarded
plastic bottles

> Somewhere along the way, we have forgotten
> how to show our appreciation for water. Water
> from the ground is polluted, and water from our
> taps no longer tastes good, so we resort to water
> in plastic bottles.

A new century, a new war, hope and despair

> Perhaps the pollution of water is nothing more
> than the pollution of the human soul. Modern
> society has gone as far as we can go. What is to
> come of us now?

Ice crystals, shining diamonds, a new hope, the
beginning of a new adventure

CONTENTS

Starting with my first collection of water-crystal photographs, *Messages from Water* [*Mizu kara no dengen*] (Vibration Kyoikusha, 1999), I have come to realize that these water books have a strange and wonderful power. They have wings of their own and go beyond my own familiar boundaries to distant lands, where they have an enormous impact. They force people to experience a different way of seeing things, and I am often invited to speak to the people who have been touched by these books.

I sometimes feel like I'm being guided by the spirit of water. I feel like I can see and even talk to this spirit, which I see as water droplets shining brightly in the air. The droplets join together to form clouds, disappearing just as fast, all for my entertainment.

Even though I now feel like I am being guided by the spirit of water, my first conscious interaction with water was not at all pleasant. In Yokohama,

Japan, where I grew up, my family lived on a plateau near the ocean. It was only a short walk down a slope to the water's edge. When the tide went out, the shallow shore was left uncovered for miles, making it a great place to hunt for various types of clams. But at high tide, the scene was completely different.

I must have been six or seven when the sea swallowed me up one day. I had gone out swimming with the boy next door, who was two years older than I.

We had gone out farther than we should have, and I suddenly began bobbing up and down, gasping for air. It was the first time I had experienced anything like it. I was only ten meters from land, but my feet didn't touch the bottom. I panicked and started waving my arms and kicking my feet. But the more I panicked, the more I sunk, and soon I started to swallow water. I thought that was going to be the end of me, but a small boat approached and pulled me out of the water.

When I went home and told my mother what had happened, she gave me some advice based on her own ability to swim and her understanding of water. "You can float if you just give in," she said. She told me that if I let the water lift me instead of trying to resist it, it would pick me up and carry me.

These words have stuck with me over the years. Since that time, I have tried to let myself go with the flow as I gently move in the direction that I wish my life to take me.

Now whenever I go swimming in the ocean or a pool, I like to just lie on my back and let myself be carried in the arms of water. And it's times like that more than any other that I feel the presence of the spirit of water in the form of shining droplets.

I feel quite confident in saying that the reason I came up with the idea of freezing water and taking photographs of the crystals was that I desired to go with the flow of life. The spirit of water came to my aid, guiding me to live the life that I now live. The spirit has led me and guided me over the years, teaching me the many things I need to know, culminating in the publication of my book *The Hidden Messages in Water*.

Shortly after its publication, readers began sending me letters of appreciation. Their kind words have helped to create a wonderful flow for me to give myself up to. Most of the letters expressed appreciation and also amazement in seeing the truth of nature revealed through water crystals.

One woman wrote, "Of all the books that I have read in my life, this is the most wonderful. Thank you so much for this book—it's as if it were surrounded by light. I will treasure it for the rest of my life."

Another message read, "To see truth revealed in such a visible way is truly surprising, amazing, and convincing. This book made me realize that the effects brought about by ancient teachings, prayer, and religion are not simply superstitions and random ideas, but effects based on the truths of the universe."

Another wrote, "My seventy-six-year-old father told me, 'Of all the books people have recommended to me, this is the only one I'm glad I read.' Thank you for this book that has changed my perspective on life."

In fact, if we were to take the energy from all these messages and make a crystal, I am certain that it would be a beautiful one.

This is the work of the water crystals. I find that those who are attracted by the beauty of crystals become connected and then they resonate with each other. Like when a single leaf falls onto the surface of water, a quiet and soft but certain wave is spreading out as a result of water's secret life being revealed to mankind.

The response has been the same all over the world. I have met with people from Germany, Switzerland, Austria, Holland, England, France, Italy, America, Canada, Costa Rica, Uruguay, Ecuador, Brazil, Australia, South Korea, the Philippines, and Taiwan, where I have given lectures. In June 2002, I was invited by the Greek Orthodox Church to join a luxury-cruise seminar tour on the Adriatic Sea along with religious leaders and scientists from around the world. Symposiums were held in Greece, Albania, Montenegro, Slovenia, Croatia, Italy, and other ports of call. Called the International Symposium on Religion, Science, and the Environment, the event was being held for the fourth time. I had been invited just three months before the symposium by one of the organizers of the symposium, a Greek woman whose daughter had showed her the collection of crystal photographs. The emotions of the many people who saw the crystal photographs reached behind the individual and resulted in a flow of wonderment from one person to another that has now became a flowing river.

There's another way to express the response to the water-crystal books. It's as if the water crystals have brought moisture back to the dried-up souls of those who live in the harsh conditions of modern society. They have replenished the brilliance of life to individuals and society. More than anything else, the photographs have succeeded in starting an enormous movement that is taking place among people around the world.

The act of living is the act of flowing. If a dam is built in a river to stop its flow, the river will die. Likewise, if the flow of blood gets dammed up somewhere in our bodies, it will mean the end of life.

The same is true for cities and countries. I was recently blessed with the opportunity to lecture to a large audience in Berlin. As you know, Berlin is a city that was once divided in two by a wall. I told the audience that just as water should remain free to flow, in no way should a city or a country be divided. The splitting of Berlin in 1961 resulted in a great hardship, loss of homes, and loss of dreams.

Then, twenty-eight years later, the wall was torn down and, like water allowed to flow freely, millions of people began to come and go of their own free will. The people emulated the flow of water, a principle of nature. And the reason is that people are mostly water.

About 70 percent of our bodies are water. This is the case for adults of all races, and it is why people should not be divided by political strategies and ideologies. Just like water, people must always be allowed to flow freely.

When I finished speaking to the audience, I noticed that a change had come over the hall. It was like a feeling spread over all of us. A wave of people stood up and started clapping. Their souls had been touched by my message, and the result was a wave of emotion that encompassed the hall, creating an ever-larger wave that would expand to others.

The desire for peace and prayers of love cannot be contained within borders. Differences in skin color or language are easily overcome when hearts resonate together, creating a new flowing wave.

A small adventure beginning with a tiny little water crystal has spread to people all over the world, creating a growing movement. The water crystals have resonated with something pure and holy deep within the souls of the people who see the photographs. Hearts have been opened, and love, gratitude, and a hope for peace have spilled out, opening the way for a new adventure.

~~~~~~

Through this book and through these crystal photographs, I hope to convey the power of prayer.

When water is exposed to certain expressions—"You're cute," "You're beautiful," "Love and gratitude"—a beautiful crystal results when the water is frozen. What does this really mean for us? The thoughts in our hearts have an impact on all life and in the creation of our world tomorrow.

A wondrous power resides within the human soul. We hear all the time that our actions are a result of our thoughts, and this principle is truly demonstrated in how water forms crystals according to what influences it has been exposed to.

But the power to affect action with thought is a double-edged sword. If people desire to see the destruction of the world, then that is what will result.

A lot has happened in our world since people have become aware of the water crystals. Gigantic buildings—symbols of civilization and prosperity—have collapsed before our eyes. New wars have erupted. We have seen sadness give birth to anger, and anger create more sadness, creating a cycle that encompasses the world around us. Some people cry, some look down in despair, and some look up in prayer. We must use the power within us to keep our thoughts focused on the good around us and not on the forces of destruction.

We are at a point in human history when we most need to rediscover some important truths that we have somehow forgotten. In fact, this might be our last chance. And this is the lesson that I feel water crystals are trying to teach us.

My research into crystals began with the desire to get even one tiny step closer to understanding the universe, but that has now led to the evolution of a broad field of study for me.

I have seen the effect that bright smiles of people throughout the world and expressions of emotion can have on the formation of beautiful crystals. But you may ask, can world peace occur from mere water crystals? It is my desire to take the first step in that direction and then one more and then another and on and on toward that end.

As I continue my conversation with water, the crystals continue to teach me many lessons: the importance of living in tune with the rhythm of life and the flow of nature, leaving the earth beautiful for future generations; love; and prayer. All of these various messages have been included in this book. I could be no happier than to find that it has had a positive influence on all those who have picked it up.

Finally, I would like to express my appreciation to Beyond Words Publishing, my English-language publisher of *The Hidden Messages in Water* and *The True Power of Water*, and all others who have helped in various ways, and also my staff at IHM who endured many hours in a refrigerated room taking pictures of crystals.

~~~~~~~~~~~~~~~

Tune in to the Hado of Happiness

What comes to mind when you think about happiness?

Do you think about love coming true for you? Perhaps the moment of birth of a son or a daughter? A job well done? Or a time you remember lying in the green grass and gazing up at the blue sky? The answer is different for everyone. We all have our own image of what happiness is. But all of us want to live a life filled with happiness.

I know of only one way to do this, and that is to align yourself with the hado of happiness. As I described in my book *The True Power of Water*, hado is the subtle energy that exists in all things.

All that exists in the universe vibrates at a unique frequency. So if you emit a hado of happiness, then you can be sure that the universe will respond with happiness. What do you need to do to align yourself with the hado of happiness?

Part of the problem is that it's hard to know what happiness really is. Perhaps there was a time when you thought you were happy, but then you realized that it was only an illusion. Or maybe you believed that a blissful relationship was finally within your reach only to compare what you had with someone else and see your dream castle crumble in the sand and be washed away.

On a trip to Germany, my daughter, who now lives in the Netherlands, told me about one of her friends who had lived in East Germany before the Berlin Wall came down. The construction of the Berlin Wall was a time of great sadness for the people of Germany, but my daughter's friend said that despite the city being divided, life on the east side of the wall went on basically as normal. In fact, a sense of contentment came from knowing that no one had to worry about what others were thinking because everyone was poor.

But when the wall finally came down and the people in the eastern part of the city were now suddenly able to obtain everything that the western part of the city had to offer, problems began. The more new, shiny things they saw, the more they wanted. But the easterners were basically still poor, so the result was a lot of unsatisfied needs. Some even longed for the days before the wall came down when people were poor and prices low.

It seemed as if the country had first been torn apart and then put back together all without regard for the will of the people. Of course the fall of the Berlin Wall is one of the most jubilant moments of modern history, but we have to admit that even this wonderful turning point had its repercussions.

When we start to compare our happiness with that of others, we soon start resonating with the hado of unhappiness. As long as we search for happiness from the outside, then it's unlikely that true happiness can ever be found.

Return to Bliss

The search for happiness is ultimately and simply a search for self. You can go searching for it in distant lands, but you'll only find it in the palm of your hand.

Think back far enough in your life and you'll probably remember a time when you felt innocent bliss. Your life had meaning and you were so busy living that time was forgotten. Then adulthood set in and you put those things away and locked the door. Perhaps you have even forgotten where you put the key.

But those happy feelings are not gone for good. With a little effort, you can open the door and take out those things that you thought were forever a part of your past. When you are true to your self and search for what you really want to be and do, your life will once again begin to flow.

In your job, in your play, and in your love, you need to return to the starting point to find the bliss. When you do this, you will soon realize that your life has changed. You'll first feel a renewed sense of health and well-being. This is because the bliss within you will purify the water that flows through your body. If we were to take a picture of such water, the resulting crystal would most certainly astound us.

One treatment suggested for people with cancer is "life-purpose treatment." By finding a purpose in life—giving speeches, climbing a mountain, laughing—the immune system is revitalized and the cancer often goes into remission. It's now common knowledge in the medical community that your mind has an enormous impact on your body. Filling your body with the hado of bliss is the very best secret for living a healthy life.

This state of bliss is also the key to expanding what we can do. We all know that if you enjoy something, then you usually excel at it. Yukio Funai, a famous business consultant in Japan who has provided advice to some three thousand companies, advocates an effective method for strengthening the abilities of companies and individuals. He calls this method the "strength-development method," and it simply involves focusing on the strengths of the company or the individual and working to expand those strengths. Weaknesses are not even considered. The result is that the strengths become stronger and the weaknesses take care of themselves.

For example, if you run a store, it's easy to focus all your attention on how to move the products that aren't selling well. But most stores will have a product that's a strong seller. For a boutique, it may be a particular style of dress; if they can focus their attention on that dress, then sales of that product and other products as well will increase. For a business to succeed, it needs to focus on what is selling well, what's most effective, and what they do best.

We see this concept reflected in the hydroponics method of growing vegetables, which makes it possible to harvest ten thousand tomatoes from a single tomato plant. How, might you ask, is such a thing possible? The answer is surprisingly simple: create a good environment for growing tomatoes.

Plants, of course, grow in soil, but with hydroponics farming, the roots grow in water infused with the nutrition that a plant requires. And because the plant doesn't need to use up energy to push its way through the soil, the roots can grow at will and easily find all the necessary nutrition. In this way, the tomato plant is able to take advantage of all its hidden potential. I remember visiting an experimental farm operated by agronomist Shigeo Nozawa, the inventor of the hydroponics method, a few years before he died and seeing the tomato plant he had grown. To put it lightly, I couldn't believe my eyes.

The same thing applies to us as humans. When you find what you do best and realize that this is where you need to focus your attention, then you will be well on your way to returning to bliss. It won't be long before you sense that your life is undergoing a change. If you know someone, perhaps a child, who is focused on a sport or a certain aspect of study, then you need to provide nourishment in the form of encouragement and compliments. This will help the person become even more focused and more determined.

A good illustration of what can result from the right words can be seen in the formation of water crystals. When water is exposed to the words "You have to do it," the result is never a well-formed crystal. This also goes for words like "You fool," and the worst, "It's no good." Perhaps it's time to take these words out of your vocabulary. Fill it instead with words like "Thank you," "Let's do it," "I love you," "Beautiful," and "Well done." Make these warm and beautiful words the ones you use the most.

The words that make beautiful crystals from the water that flows through your body are the words that fill you with a gentle feeling of peace. And that is when you will be able to expand on your abilities and go about each day with passion and bliss.

In my previous book, I explained how we put cooked rice in three glass jars, and to one of the jars we said "Fool!" To another we said "Thank you." And we simply ignored the rice in the third bottle. The rice that was told "Thank you" fermented and had quite a nice fragrance. The rice that was told "Fool!" darkened and rotted. The rice that was ignored turned black and emitted a highly repugnant smell.

However, that's not the end of the story. I took these same jars of rice to an elementary school, and the students said "Thank you" to the rice in all three containers. It wasn't long before the rice in all three containers fermented and started to emit a pleasant smell—even the rice that had spoiled.

This indicates that even that which is dying and decaying can be brought back to life by caring attention, kind words, and positive thoughts.

Shinichiro Terayama, a former director of the Japan Holistic Medical Society, is a testament to this. Terayama spent his career as an impassioned businessman, and before that he had kidney cancer. He started making it a habit to wake up early and go to the rooftop of his condominium to greet the rising sun. As he watched the morning sun each day, he began to realize that life is a gift, and the words "Thank you" started coming out of his mouth. Without turning his eyes from his cancer, he instead spoke words of appreciation to the cells, and the result was that they began to recover. The cancer receded until he was declared cured.

The ability of the spoken word to give life is much more powerful than we can imagine. A ten-year-old girl conducted an experiment similar to the rice experiment but instead used sunflower seeds. On the seed envelope, the flowerpots, and the watering can, she wrote the words "Thank you" for one and "Fool" for the other, and then she spoke these words to the respective seeds as she took care of them each day.

The plant exposed to "Thank you" grew tall with full, lush leaves. In sharp contrast, the plant exposed to "Fool" had a deformed stem and wrinkled leaves. When we looked at the plants through a microscope, we saw that the leaves of the plant exposed to "Thank you" were dense, while the other plant had leaves that appeared weak and frail.

This may well indicate the presence of consciousness in plants, accounting for this striking difference in the two plants raised by the young girl. I learned about this experiment when the mother of the young girl wrote me a letter, which she ended with a question: *What would happen if this same thing applied to raising children?*

~~~~~~

One way to look at words is to consider them the switch for turning on or off the vibration of everything in the universe. Or perhaps words can be thought of as a remote control that has the power to reach anywhere.

Humans are the only animals capable of using words, and this allows us to align our wavelength with anything and everything that exists in the universe. And it's instantaneous. Our words and our thoughts can go anywhere and to everyone in the instant they come forth.

Experiences of unexplainable coincidences are too common to be ignored. Perhaps you have dreamed about someone and later found out that they had died. Perhaps you've thought about someone from your past and then you get a call from that person. It's happened to all of us. And the cause of this phenomenon can be found in the vibration of thoughts.

I once conducted the following experiment. I filled a jar with plain water from the tap at my office in Tokyo, and then I put it on my desk. Since the water came from the city water-works system and contained chlorine, attempts to make crystals from the water failed.

I then asked for the help of five hundred people located throughout Japan. At the same time on the appointed day, they all sent positive thoughts to purify the water on my desk and then sent the message "Thank you" to the water.

As expected, the water changed and was able to form beautiful crystals. The chlorinated water from the tap had changed to pure water.

How could this have happened? I think you know the answer. The thoughts and words of five hundred people reached the water without regard for the borders of time and space.

And in the same way, the vibration of your thoughts at this very moment is having a certain effect on the world. If you understand this, then you can also understand that you already hold in your hands all the keys you need to change your life.

There Is Value in Unhappiness

We can learn another thing about happiness from the perspective of hado: Life is not all happiness. As long as there is life, there will be sadness. All our high hopes can be easily deflated, but another way to look at this is to realize that unhappiness is the path on the way to happiness.

We exposed water to the words "happiness" and "unhappiness." As expected, the water exposed to "happiness" formed beautiful round crystals that would make a precious ring. But what about crystals formed from water exposed to "unhappiness"? We expected to find deformed and broken crystals, but the crystals were rather beautiful hexagonal crystals that looked like they had been cut in half. It looked as if the water was trying its best to form crystals. It would seem, then, that unhappiness is not really the opposite of happiness. Unhappiness, in fact, is the process required for the creation of happiness.

Happiness and unhappiness are like two ends of the same rope, and sometimes you hold one end of the rope and everything goes your way, and other times you have the other end of the rope and nothing goes your way.

Such is life. We all want to be happy every day and never have to experience sadness. How unnatural that would be! Like the waves that rise and fall, if water never falls, then it could never rise or flow ahead.

For every happiness in life, there is another side. When you're in love, every day is filled with anticipation and joy, but accommodating another person in your life may require that you sacrifice your free time, your money, and your space. And you can almost be sure that after a fight, you'll find yourself thinking that you'd be better off alone. The elation felt when you buy the car of your dreams seldom lasts as long as the car. Each new scratch in the paint and each time you fork out money to maintain the car will chip away at your initial happiness.

You can never own only one side of a coin. If you want to find happiness, then you have to be ready to accept what comes with it. Such is the fate of all those who live in this world.

But we can still have hope and look forward to the future. In fact, do you think you would be able to have hope if everything went exactly as you wanted it to? Your ability to be happy no matter what and no matter when depends entirely on what's going on in your heart.

A Thankful Heart Is the Way to Happiness

Why do people go through life looking for happiness? Dogs and cats look for food and comfort, but they certainly don't go to all the trouble that people do in their continual search for happiness. I suppose the reason is that we are the only ones who can align ourselves with the hado of happiness.

Many years ago, I had a discussion with Dr. Ravi Batra, a well-known international economist, and he said something that has stuck with me:

> Why do you think people continually search for happiness? The reason is because we people have a link to unlimited existence. But many of us make a serious mistake. We set up conditions for happiness based on riches and fame, momentary pleasures, and things that are limited and always changing.
>
> There are those who are rich beyond most of our imaginations, and yet they continue to want more as they strive in vain to find happiness. The reason it's in vain is because they are looking to find unlimited happiness in limited money and riches.
>
> Unless we can become one with the unlimited existence, we will never find true happiness. This requires that we raise our consciousness.

All that can be seen with the human eye is of this limited world. Sooner or later, the material trappings will end, and as long as that is how we define happiness, our hearts will always feel hollow.

Of course I understand that casting aside all desire is not possible or even advisable. In fact, desire is not what's preventing us from finding happiness. An appropriate amount of desire is needed to make people strive for something better, and it's what made it possible for human society to rise to its current level. The problem arises when we become slaves to our desires. Our modern society operates on the ability to stir up desire in the masses.

It's no easy task to find happiness in a society established on insatiable desire. So what is it that we need to do to escape never-ending desire and find happiness? The answer is to have a thankful heart.

More than ever, we live in a time when love and appreciation is truly needed. And I think the right ratio for appreciation and love is 2:1—the exact ratio of hydrogen to oxygen in the H_2O molecule!

We have seen where words of appreciation and love result in crystals of indescribable beauty.

There are no conditions needed for appreciation. We can be thankful for life and for our freedom to move about.

When you align your soul with the hado of appreciation and love, a small drop of happiness will seep into your heart and spread throughout your body. This will link you to the vibration of happiness, and happiness will become a part of your daily life. And this is the secret for finding happiness right now wherever you are.

The Invisible World of Hado

Water crystals are just one aspect or face of the universe. Water changes its appearance at will as it attempts to speak to us concerning the formation of the cosmos. It is in itself a temporary world formed within a severe environment.

We can peer into this temporary world when we photograph crystals. To take the photographs, we collect water and place drops in fifty petri dishes. We then freeze them at minus 25 degrees centigrade and let them cool for two and a half hours, during which time they form tiny round clumps of ice. We then peer at the ice at five degrees below zero at a magnification of 200 times. The crystals appear for only two minutes under the microscope. During that time, the tiny water crystals form hexagonal patterns and then melt just as quickly as they appear.

In just a few precious moments, the door to a new dimension is opened, giving us a glimpse into a fantasy world. People who see photographs of these crystals are fascinated by their wondrous beauty. Like the kaleidoscope that we remember looking into as a child, we are suddenly carried away into another world, if only for a brief moment.

This world we enter is the invisible world of vibration, or hado. Three key words are helpful to understand hado. The first is *frequency*. The entire universe is vibrating at a particular and unique frequency. Frequency can be modeled as waves, a fact easily supported by quantum mechanics. All matter is frequency as well as particles. What this means is that rather than considering something a living organism or a mineral, something we can touch or something we can see, everything is vibrating, and vibrating at a unique and individual frequency. But that is still not all, for the words we speak, the words we write, paintings, and photographs all emit their own frequencies as well.

You may have heard of blind people who are able to "see" colors. When they hold something in their hands, they are able to *feel* the color. They know if something is a warm color or a cool color, a strong color or a pale color. Similar to how we feel the temperature and texture of an object, these people are able to feel the color through their skin. They are receptive to the unique frequency emitted by different colors.

The same applies to written words. People with psychic powers reportedly can read a word by touching it while their eyes are closed, and some say they can read letters still sealed in an envelope. If you consider the concept of hado, you might consider that there is the possibility of this being more than a parlor trick.

But why would the formation of crystals be affected by a word written on a piece of paper and placed around a beaker of water for a few hours, or a photograph placed under a beaker for twenty-four hours? The answer, I believe, is that water is capable of feeling hado from the source and memorizing it.

The second word helpful in understanding hado is *resonance*. Resonance is made possible when there is a sender of hado information and a receiver of the information. Say you make a call to someone you want to talk to. Unless that person picks up the receiver, there will be no conversation. Without a receiver, information cannot be sent. A Japanese expression *aun no kokyu*, or "in-breath and out-breath," means a state where subtle synchronization occurs when we do things together. This also refers to a relationship between a sender and a receiver.

When there is a match in vibrations, resonance occurs. We can observe the phenomenon of resonance in various aspects of daily life. For example, if you have feelings of hatred toward someone, there is a good chance that this person feels the same way about you. Likewise, if you have positive feelings toward someone, that person will sense those feelings even if you don't express them in words. What we feel in our hearts has a strange way of being relayed to other people.

The third word helpful for understanding hado is *similarity*. The macro world we know is a symbol, an expansion of the micro world. The nine rotating planets in our solar system are the macro version of the electrons circulating around the atomic nucleus, and what is going on within the human body is a miniaturization of what is going on in the grandeur of nature.

We can also say that this is an aspect of the fractal theory. When you look at a tree, you can see that the tips of the branches divide and spread out much in the same way that the first branches of the tree divide and spread out. In other words, because the tree is formed in the same way as the branches, the tree forms a single silhouette, which is sometimes called a fractal structure. The fractal structure can be seen in various aspects of nature: in the ocean coast, in the churning of a river, and in the formation of clouds.

This is also the case with water crystals. Why do water crystals form hexagonal shapes? When the molecules of water join together, the hexagonal shape is the most stable. Of course, such hexagonal structures are too small to see, but when these small structures join together, they form a larger hexagonal shape. In other words, the placement of molecules too small to see and the formation of crystals that we can see through our microscopes are in compliance with the fractal structure.

So by observing the micro world, we can increase our understanding of the macro world; likewise, by observing macro phenomenon, we can learn more about the micro world.

These three key words—*frequency*, *resonance*, and *similarity*—will give you a better understanding of hado. Another important aspect of hado is flow. The Buddha, knowing that flow is a fundamental principle of the universe, said that all things are in flux and nothing is permanent. Water is a good example of this. Water is always flowing with life, purifying what it encounters as it travels. It carries with it the nourishment necessary for sustaining life while also carrying away impurities, giving life to all.

All life flows with the flow of water. Even your life is in constant flow with water. In fact, even the cycle of birth and death complies with this single principle. Circulation is indeed the law of nature.

But there is one form of life that insists on breaking this law of nature: humankind. The desire for more, pride, and the insistence of one ideology over another all serve to block the flow. This is the cause of many of the problems that we find ourselves facing in these troubled times. War that begets greed, tragedy that begets loathing, pollution that begets apathy. These are distortions or blockages of the natural ways of nature.

Many of the problems that we have not even started to solve require careful resolve and bold action. And what will be necessary for us to arrive at solutions? The answer is circulation. This is the key that we need to open the floodgates to a new day for the human race—finding happiness, spreading love, restoring peace, and protecting this jewel called Earth. It all begins with circulation, and it is water that will show us the way. I invite you to begin the journey:

Let's listen carefully. Let's listen to the voice of water.

And steep ourselves in the fantasy world created by water crystals.

Someday we will return to water and become a part of the natural flow.

Filled with amazement, your heart and your step will be lightened.

Such a feeling will show you the most beautiful sight you've ever seen.

There's no need to resist the flow.

No need to be afraid of moving forward.

And the reason is that you are water.

Water's Healing Melody

If you find yourself feeling down, over-whelmed by the daily grind, or offended by an unkind word or act, then I suggest you try something: simply look at water. Walk to the edge of a nearby pond or a stream and cast your eyes on the gentle waves reflecting the sun. If it's raining, find a puddle and watch the raindrops make rings that appear and disappear. Or while you are washing dishes at the sink, gaze at the geometric creations made as the light from the window mingles with water cascading downward.

I recommend this because you will discover that water takes you to another world where you will feel the water within being washed clean; you will be able to return to who you really are. You have just forgotten for a while that you are water. As you let the water flow gently through your mind and your body, it will heal you at your core.

The flow of water has much to teach us. In fact, the act of living is the act of flowing. It's almost as if the water within your body has a desire to flow. In the same way, your soul must also flow. When your soul is allowed to flow, you feel a burden lifted from your weary body, for the soul and the body are simply two sides of the same coin.

If you have been offended, forgive the offender. And if you feel oppressed for your own offenses against others, forgive yourself. Forgiveness opens up the path for you to naturally and freely flow toward your future.

The universe holds something potentially wonderful for you at each passing moment of life. Open yourself to the good things flowing toward you and you will be able to reach out and welcome a wonderful future into your bosom. If you can't get over a broken heart no matter how hard you try, the last thing you can do is go back and change the past. But there always remains the possibility that the flow of life will take you to a place more wonderful than you could have hoped for. Every second of life is a new crossroads with new possibilities. If you can realize this, you can free yourself from your burdens, you will see how trivial your problems are, and you will no longer need to be tied to the past.

Water teaches us how to live, how to forgive, how to believe. If you open your ears to the possibilities in life, you may just be able to hear the sound of the pure water that flows through your body even now. It is the sound of your life—a melody of healing.

Water Is Part of the Rhythm of Life

The water flowing within us is part of the water flowing through nature and part of the rhythm of life being played out throughout the universe.

In Europe and other parts of the world, it has long been said that the moon rules over water. The ocean's tides are directly affected by the movements of the moon. Perhaps low and high tides are the most visible response to the moon, but wherever life is to be found, there is certain to be a link to the movement of the moon. The clam feels the gravitational pull from the moon and opens its shell at high tide. The breeding cycle of the sea urchin is exactly in line with the lunar cycle. And seagulls come to shore to lay their eggs almost always on the evening of a full moon, for reasons other than the increased light.

We could hardly expect that human bodies, consisting of 70 percent water, would be the exception. More babies are born when there is a full moon, as any midwife will tell you. The female reproductive cycle is in time with the moon's. Many people with sharpened sensitivities say they are energized on nights when the moon is full. Full-moon energy is linked to insanity and stories of werewolves. Even the word *lunatic* comes from the root *lunar*.

It makes perfect sense that most of the ancient cultures of the world have relied on the lunar calendar to measure time. The lunar calendar, which is closely aligned with the cycle of life, was an important tool for planting and harvesting crops.

When our rhythm is in line with the movement of the moon, we can more easily align to the flowing of the water within us. This is nothing less than living life to the beat of the drum played by the rhythm of nature. It is also a piece of wisdom mostly lost on modern man.

Similar to the lunar calendar is the thirteen-month calendar used by the Mayans, which is somewhat different from the lunar calendar. I learned about Dr. Jose Arguelles and his wife, Lloydine, who have made it their cause to print copies of this calendar and spread its use throughout the world. They believe that if the calendar is used on a global scale, then people will start to live within the rhythm of nature, thus opening paths that lead to solutions for many of the problems faced by modern society.

According to this calendar, the new year starts on July 26. When the 365 days of the year are divided by 28, the days in each month, you get 13 months. And one extra day. On the Mayan calendar, this extra day of the year was called "the day out of time." All work was laid aside, prayers were offered, and prosperity was celebrated with laughter and dance.

While changing to a lunar-based calendar may not be practical or desirable for everyone, we can attune to the moon and the rhythm of life in our own ways. The human body is a tiny universe of its own. Being in tune with this grand universe within allows us to fully experience the energy flowing from the cosmos. When we return to living as one with the universe, we will rediscover the simplicity and spontaneity we were intended for and that was intended for us.

The number of people in the world searching for inner healing is vast, and it may include you. Perhaps the reason is because the environment we have created for ourselves has evolved too fast, and now we find ourselves in a world of pain and fatigue of our own creation. How do we save ourselves from it? Listen to the melody flowing from the world around you. When you can feel this rhythm flowing within the water that makes up your being, then you will become one with the water crystals. This is the life that so many of us are searching for. It's the healing experience that we know deep in our souls is waiting for us. Everyone is searching for healing.

Music as a Healing Force

Alan Roubik is an American pianist who has based his musical career on the principle that music has the ability to heal. In addition to being a performer, Alan is a music producer for television commercials and films, and he also has his own recording company. His piano music has no rival in clarity: many who listen to it say that they feel like their bodies become transparent.

Alan had an experience when he was a young boy which convinced him that music has the power to heal, and since that time, he has based his career on writing music for healing. He started playing the organ at age three as a child prodigy, and from the age of nine, he focused on the piano and on writing and performing. But in his teen years his life took a sudden change. He injured the ulnar nerve in his right arm during physical-education class at school, making it painful and nearly impossible to move his fingers.

For several months, he was unable to play the piano. The muscles in his fingers began to weaken. It seemed as if the road to his future had suddenly come to an insurmountable impasse, and the realization that he would likely lose the music which he loved so much sent him into a deep depression. He tried thinking about other futures, but he always found himself sitting in front of the piano.

And then one day, perhaps in utter desperation, he put his hands on the keyboard and let whatever was in his heart come out. Alan says that what he felt at that moment was something like happiness in his fingers. He could feel the life energy flowing through his hands and the resonance between the sound of the piano and the movement of his fingers.

Alan's hands began to recover almost immediately, and it wasn't long before he was able to play as good as before—or even better.

I first met Alan in 1995 through an introduction by the scientist who had invented the Magnetic Resonance Analyzer (MRA), a hado measuring instrument that is capable of measuring minute vibrations. With the cooperation of this scientist, we asked Alan to compose music that would express the healing powers of hado. We wanted to have healing music that would be capable of boosting the body's immune system.

When the score was completed and recorded, we exposed water to it, and as might have been expected, crystals formed from the water were exceedingly beautiful and delicate—typical of healing characteristics.

When we showed photographs of the crystals to Alan, he said that he was surprised to see that all the crystals formed were identical to the images he had in his mind when he was composing the music.

Alan is one of many artists who is highly aware that music is a form of healing. But we also know that the classical music from the past, famous jazz pieces, and folk music from the corners of the world also have the ability to heal in their own individual ways.

I exposed water to classical music from various composers and then took photographs of the resulting crystals. Then we took hado measurements of the photographs with the MRA. The results revealed the hado—emotional and physical—affected by the music. Some of these results I shared in *The True Power of Water*. Here are two additional findings:

Wagner's "Ride of the Valkyries"
> Emotional hado: Self-pity
> Physical hado: Alleviation of indirect
> pain

Debussy's "Prelude to 'The Afternoon of
a Faun'"
> Emotional hado: Environmental stress
> Physical hado: Alleviation and preven-
> tion of back problems

What this all means is that good music has the ability to guide us on the path of healing. It seems that this is especially the case with classical music, which has stood the test of time. When water is exposed to this music, my research has found that the water becomes energetic, and beautiful crystals are formed.

Music is also a representation of the time and environment in which the music was composed. If you look back on different periods in history, you'll find that different periods are characterized by certain music. This is because the types and degrees of stress that society experiences change with the times and require healing. This results in the creation of music that harmonizes with the frequency prevalent in society.

Consider the jazz that came out of New York beginning in the 1940s. Toru Yazawa, a member of a popular band in Japan known as Alice, once shared with me a brief history of jazz.

Jazz got its start with the blues sung and played by African-Americans. When this music was combined with the brass bands of New Orleans, the result was the vivid and liberal genre known as New Orleans jazz. The jazz of this period was mostly simple three-chord melodies, which is why it sounds simple and blissful.

Over time, the center of jazz moved to New York, and in the years after the end of World War II, a new form of jazz called modern jazz started to emerge. Modern jazz consists of complicated chords. Sounds that would normally create a roar were combined, and then other sounds are piled on top of each other, resulting in the uniquely gloomy, avant-garde feel of modern jazz.

During that time, New York City, as well as the whole United States, was experiencing uneasiness and anxiety over the emergence of the Soviet Union and other threatening enemies, creating the atmosphere that led to the Korean and Vietnam wars. Those who lived in New York, a melting pot of different people, in that particular time were experiencing a type of stress never felt before. Perhaps, simpler music (three-chord) was needed for healing simpler human relations, while more complex music was needed for healing more complex human relations. Simply put, music, in addition to being art and providing entertainment, is more than anything a form of healing.

Healing with Hado

As I mentioned in my book *The True Power of Water*, I am keenly interested in the field of hado medicine. Hado medicine focuses on the underlying cause of the symptoms of illness, in contrast to the medical practices which require that we take pills or undergo surgery to deal with symptoms of disease. Hado medicine deals with the unique vibration of the illness itself. I can say with certainty that the day will come when hado medicine is widely accepted. Most people today go to the drugstore to find solutions for their ailments, but perhaps one day instead of getting a prescription of medicine, you will get a prescription of music to heal what's ailing you. Such a day may not be as far away as you think.

All symptoms of illnesses vibrate at a unique frequency. By knowing the frequency, it is possible to overlap the exact opposite wavelength on top of the symptom's wavelength; thus, the frequency of the illness is dissipated and the symptoms are alleviated. This is already in practice to some degree with treatment for Parkinson's disease and other neurological illnesses.

Hado medicine not only deals with the specific body part where symptoms are located; it also helps to alleviate the real cause behind the sickness, which is often negative emotions. For example, if a person is experiencing liver problems, then we will also almost always find that the person has anger issues. The wavelength generated by anger is the same as the wavelength generated by the molecules of the cells that make up the liver, so the wavelengths of anger and the liver are in tune with each other. In the same way, the emotion of sadness is in tune with the blood, and so sad people tend to be easily plagued by leukemia and hemorrhage-type strokes. Continued irritability damages the nervous system, often leading to pain, sensitivity, and stiff muscles in the lower neck and shoulders.

An important aspect of hado medicine is that the human body is considered to be a universe of its own. Our bodies consist of some 60 trillion cells, each carrying out its specialized responsibility while simultaneously harmonizing with other cells in a wonderful way to make us who we are. The organs, nerves, and cells of the body have their own unique frequency. The body is like a grand orchestra consisting of the harmonization of various sounds. When something goes wrong somewhere in our body, there is discord with one of the sounds. And when even one sound is out of pitch, the entire composition is not as it should be.

A dentist named Kazumasa Muratsu has seen significant results with patients he has treated based on the perspective that teeth are nothing less than organs of the body. In one instance, one of his patients was unable to clench her hands for many years, but when Dr. Muratsu removed the metal fillings on her upper teeth and adjusted her bite, she regained full use of her hands. She also found that she no longer suffered from chronic pain in her lower back and her right leg.

This indicates that teeth have an effect on the entire body, and complications with teeth can influence the rest of the body in totally unpredictable ways. Dr. Muratsu, in fact, says that the teeth are one part of the core control center of the body.

But modern medicine sees the human body as a machine consisting of various independent parts, and the healing they provide deals only with taking care of the particular defect of the particular part that's gotten out of order. But if one symptom is attended to and followed by something failing elsewhere in the body, then true healing has not really taken place. Hado medicine is all about dealing with the health of the entire body, which is why the word *healing* and not "curing" is more appropriate.

Other Forms of Hado Medicine

We can see that hado medicine holds tremendous promise, but I don't want to give you the impression that this technology is anything new. The principles were well known by the ancient cultures and incorporated into their daily lives. In fact, there have been many cases where the wisdom of the distant past has been reexamined to discover that the applications are still valid in our day.

The use of flower essences is one ancient method of healing that has paved the way for hado medicine. The energy and vibration of flowers is transferred to water, and by drinking this water, the patient receives both physical and mental healing benefits. You might postulate that during the transferring process, it is the actual components of the flower that are dissolved in the water, but actually it is only the vibration that gets transferred. Therefore, a chemical analysis of flower essence will detect only water.

The science of flower essence was established by a British bacteriologist named Dr. Edward Bach. He developed essences known as Bach Flower Remedies, which can now be found throughout the world. In fact, flower essence therapy has expanded to incorporate the characteristics of individual countries. A popular form of flower essence in Japan is called Findhorn flower essence. In northern Scotland, near Loch Ness Lake, there is a community called Findhorn where people from all over the world have come together to live and participate in events and workshops related to living as one with nature and finding one's true way through life.

Marion Leigh introduced flower essence therapy at Findhorn. She is a woman whose smile has the brilliance of flowers. I interviewed Marion when she came to Japan several years ago. She told me,

> Our bodies serve as a tool for accomplishing spiritual missions. In order to carry out our mission, we need to release the warped feelings and emotions—fear and grief, sadness, suspicion, impatience, weaknesses, and apathy—that form a block between the spirit and the body.
>
> Such emotions become the cause of many of the symptoms that we experience. Our modern medicine is for the most part unable to deal with the roots of our illnesses, but this is an area where flower essence has proven to be effective.

According to Veda philosophy from India, there are seven places on the human body called chakra points that serve as the portals for unseen energy to enter the body. It is said that flower essence makes use of these chakras to heal certain ailments and parts of the body, depending on the characteristics of the flower. The gorse flower prevalent around the area of Findhorn has a vibration of joy and passion and can be used to effectively deal with a lack of energy, depression, and the weakening of the immune system. Scottish primrose is a symbol of peace and is used to calm and harmonize during times of fear or panic. The cherry blossom can be made into an essence that has the ability to return you to your inner path. It can effectively be used to help you overcome negative patterns of thinking and feelings of inferiority that weigh you down, while helping you to regain feelings of love and compassion.

To make your own flower essence, go outside on a bright and sunny morning and collect flowers. Cut each flower at the stem, being careful not to touch the flower itself with your hand. Then put the flowers in a container filled with fresh and pure water and set it in the sun. In about four hours, the essence of the flower will be transferred to the water. You can add a little brandy to make the water last longer. Store the water in glass bottles, and as you use it, dilute it even more with water. As needed, put a few drops on your tongue. Your body and soul will feel the effect without the typical side effects of modern medicine.

I decided to see what would happen if I diluted such essence and made crystals. The crystals that resulted were all very beautiful, not unlike the flowers themselves.

~~~~~

Vibration is something you can't see with the naked eye, which is why it is difficult to verify the positive effects of hado healing using modern analysis and medical examinations. However, we shouldn't be too quick to say that there can be no benefits without scientific verification. Many recognized home remedies do in fact make use of the principle of vibration. Homeopathy, as a form of vibration-based medicine, has the ability to heal the body by using vibrational water.

Homeopathy is a medicine in which "like cures like." To treat an illness, the poison that causes the symptom is diluted with water by 10 to the power of 10, and sometimes even by 10 to the power of 600 or more. The poison, diluted to almost an incomprehensible level, is then given to the patient.

Lacquer, for example, often causes a rash when it comes in contact with skin, but when a homeopathic remedy is made using lacquer, it can be used to treat rashes and skin injuries. Freshly cut onions cause tears and a runny nose, but a homeopathic remedy made with onions is good for treating colds, hay fever, and some allergies that have symptoms of teary eyes and a runny nose. This is referred to as "the law of similars."

Homeopathy got its start when a German doctor named Samuel Hahnemann noticed that the essence of the bark of the cinchona calisaya, which is used to treat malaria, brings on symptoms of malaria when extracted and taken orally. Hahnemann developed his theory of homeopathy and announced it in the early part of the nineteenth century; thereafter homeopathy gradually spread throughout Europe and the United States. This was a completely new type of medicine, and it was widely prescribed because of the noticeable benefits.

By the middle of the nineteenth century, more than four hundred homeopathy clinics existed; even physicians to the royal family in England started practicing homeopathy in 1830. In America, homeopathy was so popular by around 1900 that one in five physicians specialized in it. But then medical associations began to form with the intention of getting rid of homeopathy practices. Such organizations, hand in hand with pharmaceutical companies, brought enormous pressure to bear, and soon homeopathy was forgotten.

This is just one more example of how the most beneficial things often receive the most negative pressure. But while homeopathy was once cast aside, it is again starting to regain its former reputation. Homeopathy is now taught in thirty or more medical schools in England, and state-operated hospitals now specialize in it. In France, homeopathic remedies can be purchased at the neighborhood drugstore; about 10 percent of German doctors are homeopathic physicians. In recent years, a homeopathy medical association has been established in Japan, and more and more people are becoming aware of the benefits of this practice.

Healing Comes in Unexpected Forms

Two hundred years ago homeopathy was recognized as an effective form of medicine, and many people over the years can testify to its effectiveness. But it goes mostly unrecognized by modern medicine. I know of one well-known scientific journal that has featured article after article supporting the benefits of homeopathy, but the articles, often published with a note of derision from the editor, have gone mostly ignored.

Many in the scientific community would say, "We know that a lot of people use it, but there is no scientific proof for the benefits of homeopathy." If homeopathy had no benefits, don't you think it would have been forgotten a long time ago?

I will be the first to admit that saying that water has the ability to read and memorize information turns scientific common sense on its head. But such unscientific phenomenon are more common than we may think.

Dr. Teruo Higa, a professor at Ryukyu University in Okinawa, has been striving to spread the use of a form of organic bacteria he developed called Effective Microorganism (EM). EM is a liquid formed from bacteria. It has been shown to be perfectly safe—even beneficial—for people and the environment. When EM is applied to soil, the result is a bountiful crop without the use of chemicals or synthetic fertilizers. When used to treat polluted water, the water becomes drinkable. It can even be used to treat the dioxin resulting from the burning of refuse.

While Dr. Higa was doing research on EM, he had a strange experience. He poured the EM liquid in a ceramic container, poured it out, and then cleaned the container, but the properties of EM persisted. He washed the container repeatedly, but he couldn't get rid of the EM properties. He tried to sterilize the container with high heat, but even that failed to eliminate the EM properties.

This gave Dr. Higa an idea. He transferred the EM into a new ceramic container. At 700 degrees centigrade, a temperature that certainly would allow no life form to survive, the bacteria survived and became baked into the ceramic. This goes against scientific common sense, but EM ceramic has proven to work and now has various uses in the home (such as water treatment and building materials), in the environment, and in agriculture.

We can say that this is another indication of hado science. All matter has its own hado, and water relays this information. The molecules of water carry messages like the magnet of a computer disk. Hado can be either beneficial for life or harmful for life. But even if the vibration is good for life, if water—the mediator—is impure, the hado will not be relayed correctly.

Dr. Higa asserts that in nature there exists both a flow of revival and a flow of destruction. For example, if a piece of fruit is left sitting, it will soon rot and emit a foul smell. This is the flow in the direction of destruction. But fermentation is the flow of revival. Fermentation is a process that creates sauerkraut, yogurt, bean-paste soup, soy sauce, cheese, liquor, and many other foods. Both fermenting and rotting are the work of microorganisms, but they are not the same.

EM is a collection of microorganisms that do the work of revival. When EM is added to the soil, it enhances the power of existing microorganisms; the result is high-quality vegetables without chemicals or synthetic fertilizer. EM is completely safe for humans, and it doesn't deplete the soil.

In contrast, consider chemicals and synthetic fertilizers. Chemicals do eliminate harmful insects, and synthetic fertilizers do ensure bigger crops. But their use kills even the good insects along with all the microorganisms that would normally enrich the soil. Chemicals provide instant gratification, but the long-term and lasting result is destruction of the soil. In fact, much of the farm soil now in use is, according to most definitions, lifeless. We alone have the power and responsibility for restoring the cycle of nature.

~~~~~

Many aspects of our modern society appear to be in destruction mode. For the pursuit of momentary pleasure and convenience, the cyclical laws of nature have been ignored and replaced by the convenience of use-once-and-throw-away.

And we are beginning to hear the groaning from our tortured planet. We are at a point when we must realize that if we want to continue to call this planet our home, we need to change—not the planet, but ourselves.

We have to stop being agents of destruction and start becoming agents of revival. The slogan "From a destructive-type human being to a revival-type human being" may be added to our list of slogans by which we will live from now on.

One of the most beautiful sights you'll find in Japan is a group of tiny islands not far from Hiroshima. Starting in 1998, the people who lived on the islands got together and decided they had to do something about the polluted water that surrounded them. Batches of EM were made and distributed to each home by volunteers with instructions to put it in their drains. The results were immediate and unmistakable. The clumps of sludge along the shore disappeared and schools of fish began to return. There are now octopuses and abundant clams, something that had existed only in the memories of the oldest inhabitants. The area is known for its seaweed crop, and when EM was added to the water used to wash off the harvested seaweed inland, sludge in the ditches and waterways was soon gone, and even the seaweed quality improved.

A nearby village called Akitsucho heard about the success, and they also distributed EM for free to the villagers, and again the effects were immediate. The waterways became clean, frogs returned, and clams started appearing in the once-barren bay.

The waters near Akitsucho produce some of the best oysters in Japan. When the town's residents put clods of dirt containing EM into the oyster beds, the quality of the ocean water improved, resulting in bigger and better crops than in recent memory. The use of EM spread quickly along the coast, culminating with the formation of the Seto Inland Sea Environment Conservation Council in 2002.

The people along the coast have taken the first important step to restore the revival and circulating type of society. Healing isn't only about the recovery of our own physical health. We need to think about the healing of the land, the rivers, the oceans, and the planet in its entirety.

But what does healing the planet really mean? The answer is a return to the circle of life—the circulation of resources, of water, and of life. That is our responsibility as occupants of this delicate and crystal-like planet.

Cycles of Water, Cycles of Life

According to a theory first proposed by Luis Frank at Ohio State University, and confirmed by NASA and the University of Hawaii, water arrived on this earth after traveling through space. In every minute of the day, about twelve comets, some as heavy as 100 tons, fall to earth. These comets are made up mostly of ice. When the ice reaches the atmosphere, it forms clouds and eventually falls to earth in the form of rain to fill the ocean. And since we are mostly water, in a sense we all come from outer space.

You've probably gone outside on a clear night to lie on your back and look up at the stars. Did you ever experience a feeling like nostalgia, maybe memories of long ago? When you gaze at the heavens, your soul is taken back in time millions and billions of years. Do you ever get the feeling that you yourself are somehow floating up there in the cosmos, like a planet of one? It makes a lot of sense that we would be so eternally and universally enchanted by the heavens.

From the time when Yuri Gagarin, the Russian cosmonaut, first broke the earthly shackles in 1961, and Neil Armstrong made one giant leap for mankind, the possibility that you and I might someday make the journey ourselves has steadily become more of a reality.

Scientists currently have their sights set on Mars. NASA is already working on concrete plans to send a manned spaceship to Mars, paving the way for people like you and me to become aliens on a distant planet.

But traveling to Mars presents several challenges, and here again, the solution may well be found in water. Among the risks of space travel is the weakening of muscle and bone due to the lack of gravity, not to mention the mental stress of spending long periods in isolation. Cosmic radiation is another problem. Space is filled with radiation from distant universes as well as from the solar flares of the sun, which can be especially harmful. Safe space travel requires close observation of the sun and a way to escape the intense radiation as needed. Such a place would need thick and sturdy walls.

One way that NASA is addressing this obstacle is by working on building a room in a spaceship with walls made of columns of water. The water could be used for consumption and for preparing water-based foods—and for protection. When a solar flare occurs, the water in the columns would act as a shield for the voyagers until the danger passes.

Because the weight of a spaceship must be kept to a minimum, only a limited amount of water can be carried. The average person uses about 180 liters of water a day; on a space vessel, this amount can be reduced to 3 liters. But even that small amount would add up quickly for a crew on a long journey. This is where recycling of water becomes an important issue. Systems are now being developed to effectively recycle the water used for drinking and bathing and even to recycle sweat and urine.

When the NASA probe *Odyssey* touched down on Mars in May 2001, they discovered that large volumes of water existed in the form of ice just beneath the planet's surface, meaning that water existed on the surface of the planet at some period in the distant past. If this frozen water can be used, then it opens up the possibility that this planet can be made green like our own so that people can someday inhabit it. Work is now moving ahead to make this a possibility.

In 1996, NASA conducted an experiment on Devon Island in Canada to simulate life on Mars. The experiment studied biological scenarios, living conditions, and telecommunications. The temperature on Devon Island is low and the land is barren, not unlike the environment of Mars. Scientists were studying the feasibility of space colonization, but there are other implications of the experiment. Our planet is deteriorating at a rapid rate, and no one has a definitive solution for global warming, overpopulation, starvation, pollution, and water

The two-minute life span of a water crystal is revealed through photographs.

The drama of life is played out in just two minutes, between the time the crystal forms and when it disappears.

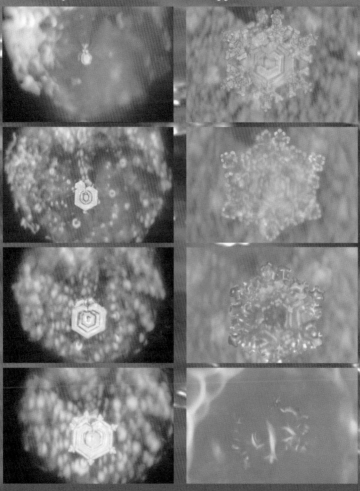

A small white granule forms on the tip of the frozen water droplet. In a brief moment, a crystal jewel appears under the microscope and then melts away.

Words are reflected in the water.
We showed words to water in a glass beaker.

Happiness

A crystal of almost perfect shape is formed, like an exquisitely cut diamond. Perhaps this tells us that balance is an important condition for happiness.

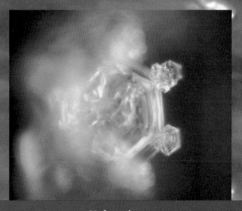

Unhappiness

This faint and weak crystal is out of balance and appears as if it is only partially formed. Unhappiness is not the opposite of happiness—it's what we experience on the way to happiness.

Hang in there.

Just the way you are.

"Hang in there" results in a rather tight and shrunk crystal. But "Just the way you are" results in a unique shape that seems to be stretching out, just as these words let an individual expand.

You're beautiful.

Try to be beautiful.

"You're beautiful" results in a beautiful, natural crystal. "Try to be beautiful" is slightly deformed. This indicates that praise yields better results than pressure.

Like

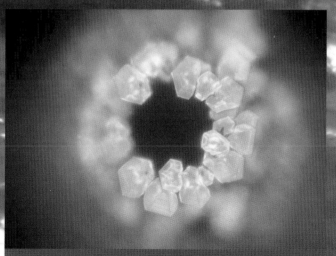

Hate

The word "Like" seems to take on the shape of a joyous heart, and "Hate" results in a hollow image, almost appearing to suffocate.

Power

Helplessness

"Power" created a crystal that was unique but jumbled; not every problem can be solved with power. "Helplessness" results in a hollow-looking crystal robbed of its power.

Innocence

Doing things with innocence perhaps gives you the greatest power to accomplish them. The crystal became too large to fit inside the frame, and so we decreased the magnification to take this picture.

Thank you

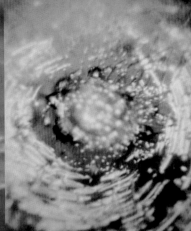

You idiot!

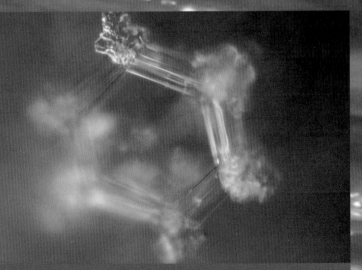

Thank you and You idiot!

When the two words in the top two photographs from my previous book were combined, the result was a thin half-formed crystal. This might indicate that the power of "Thank you" is stronger than "You idiot!"

"Thank you" in Malaysian

"Thank you" in Tagalog

"Thank you" in Portuguese

As in my previous book, we looked at the results of "Thank you" in various languages. The crystal for Malaysian was especially unique. "Thank you" in various languages has different nuances, resulting in highly distinctive crystals.

War

Peace

The crystal resulting from "War" was taken two months before September 11, 2001. The crystal looks almost as if a jet plane crashed into it. The word "Peace" creates a crystal resembling people coming together in harmony.

New York City, September 11, 2001

The events of September 11, 2001, shocked the world. The water
formed a crystal like a terrible nightmare.

Coexistence

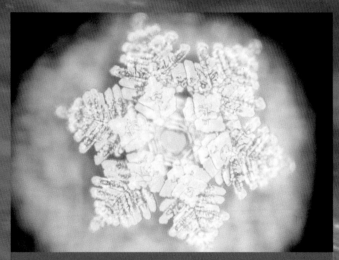

Competition

The word "Coexistence" resulted in a crystal formed by two crystals, and the word "Competition" created a surprisingly beautiful crystal. This may indicate that wholesome competition is a positive thing.

Peace of mind

"Peace of mind" created an expansive crystal. Perhaps this is what people in these hectic times need more than anything else. This is a photograph you might want to put in your pocket and carry around with you.

The god of happiness and wealth

The god of poverty

In Japan, the Shinto religion observes hundreds of deities; these are two of them. The top crystal is full and round, while the bottom one is pointed. I interpret the message to mean that if you live your life harshly like the pointed tip in the bottom picture, happiness and wealth may not come.

Marital love

This crystal may represent the relationship dynamic at work when one partner is caring and the other needful. Of course, it's best when each partner takes turns caring for the other.

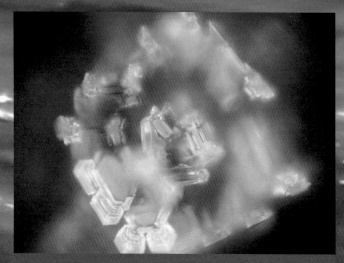

Goods and capital

Oil

These are some of the forces that move the modern economy. They are not bad in and of themselves, but when balance is lost, chaos results.

Hemp

As I discuss in chapter 5, hemp has great potential and can be used to make various products, like food and clothing, with its good vibration.

Healing melodies that touch the heart

This music has the power to heal, as seen in the formation of beautiful crystals.

Alan Roubik's "Keys to My Heart" (1–6)

Alan is doing research into the healing effects of music, and crystals formed while being exposed to his music are all beautiful. This attests to his music's healing influence.

Mendelssohn's "Wedding March"

This crystal results from the joyful wedding march. The crystal brings to mind a flower in full bloom, resembling a beautiful bride.

Wagner's "Ride of the Valkyries"

Sarasate's "Zigeunerweisen"

These are two composers from the second half of the nineteenth century. Although the motifs are different, both crystals shine with a brilliant healing effect.

Albinoni's Adagio

Schubert's "Ave Maria"

The first crystal is the reflection of a mournful melody, while the second one, reflecting "Ave Maria," is a balanced crystal that appears to be overflowing with love.

"Edelweiss," from *The Sound of Music*

Edelweiss in German means "noble white," and so appears the crystal.
We can imagine a glass mirror within the crisp white crystal.

"Amazing Grace"

This famous prayerful gospel hymn from America created a striking crystal full of grandeur and reverence.

A Celtic folk song

We played a song sung by Enya, who is an Irish singer of Celtic spirit. The resulting crystal was pure, innocent, and white, just like her voice.

"Rokudan," traditional Japanese melody played on the koto

"Hyojo Etenraku," ancient Japanese court music

These two pieces of traditional Japanese instrumental music we played to water yielded beautiful and orderly crystals, indicating overlapping tones of koto (above) and orderliness of the court music (below).

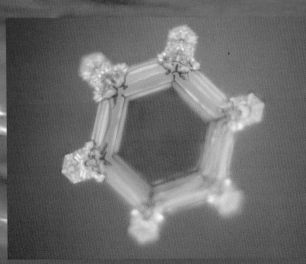

"Crane and Turtle," traditional Japanese kouta song

"The Green of Pine," traditional Japanese nagauta song

These pieces are traditional Japanese vocal music. It was interesting to see a turtle-like shape as the title indicates (above). "The Green of Pine" is a song about a beautiful prostitute.

The power of prayer can change the world.

Crystals produced before and after prayers were offered for the water and the world are dramatically different, as can be seen from these examples.

Water prayed for by five hundred people

At the same time, five hundred people from all over Japan said a prayer of love for the water. It was normal tap water, which does not usually form crystals due to the chlorine, but the water formed beautiful crystals. Feelings of love have an instantaneous effect, no matter the distance or the source of the water.

A Sanskrit prayer

This crystal resulted from a prayer to Shiva. The pattern, as balanced and orderly as a mandala, is divine indeed.

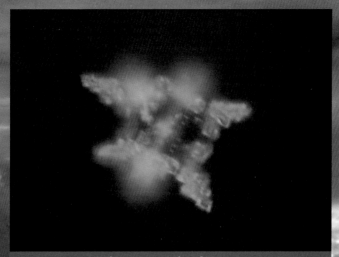

Before prayer, Lake of Lucerne

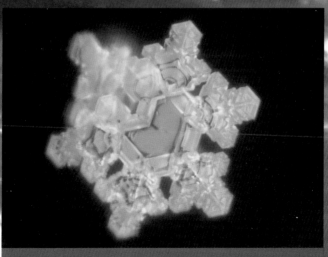

After prayer, Lake of Lucerne

We offered a Swiss Lutheran prayer at Lake of Lucerne. The crystal formed after the prayer resulted in a marked difference.

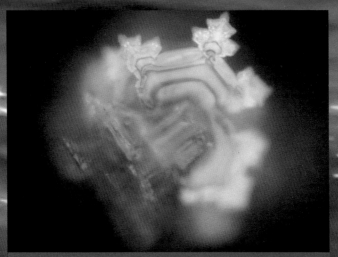

Before prayer, Lake Zurich in Switzerland

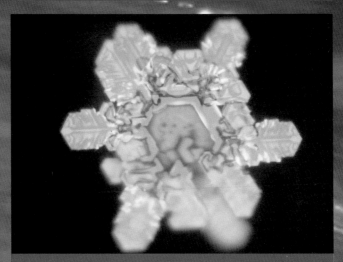

After prayer, Lake Zurich in Switzerland

At Lake Zurich in Switzerland, the crystal formed before the prayer was deformed, but the one formed after was gorgeous.

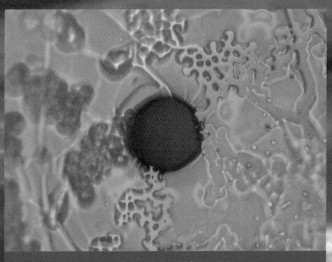

Before prayer, Bahamas

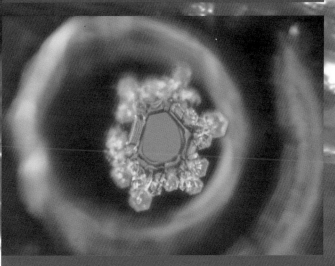

After prayer, Bahamas

We clasped our hands around a cup of water on the table and spoke to the water with feelings of prayer, resulting in a completely different crystal.

Before prayer, Uchi Lake, Oklahoma

During prayer, Uchi Lake, Oklahoma

After prayer, Uchi Lake, Oklahoma

We gathered people who lived near Uchi Lake in Oklahoma and had them offer a prayer for the water. It's easy to see how the crystal changed from the prayer.

shortages. It makes one wonder how long our own planet will remain friendly and inhabitable. Will we someday be faced with the realization that the only way we will survive as a species is by moving to a distant planet such as Mars? It is no small problem. Understanding water's remarkable journey to and through our planet may bring us closer to the answers we are searching for.

Water's Adventures on Planet Earth

Imagine you have just returned from a trip into space. You step off your vessel onto our green planet and find yourself standing in a deep green forest. Rays of light filter through the trees towering above you. Fallen leaves soften the ground, and deep-green moss envelops the trunk of a fallen tree. Ferns cover the ground all around you. The sounds of life permeate the air—the flapping of wings, the calling of birds, and the wind whistling through the trees and shaking the leaves. As you take a deep breath of cool air and let the scents of pristine nature fill your body, you have a deep realization that this is your planet and your birthright. And that is why you must love it and why you do.

You now see water trickling out between rocks, forming a pool of water. You cup your hands together and drink. You feel the energy of the earth filling your soul, and you know it's because of all that water has experienced in its secret life.

Where did this water, arising from the bosom of the earth, come from? Think for a moment about the earth as water has experienced it. Arriving from the cosmos in the form of clumps of ice, water fell from the sky upon mountains and forests to give moisture to the trees. That first droplet of dew on a leaf is water in its infancy. From there it begins a journey of unforeseen adventures on our planet. After water falls in the form of rain, what happens next?

A good portion of rainwater—one-third of all that falls—seeps into the ground where it's absorbed by plants, again to be evaporated into the atmosphere. In evergreen forests, as much as ten tons of water will evaporate from a square hectare (approximately 2½ acres) in the first few moments after a downpour.

The water will then rise into the air as mist that drifts among the trees, or it will rise even higher to form clouds. Water in the form of mist will sometimes take another path. When the temperature drops below the freezing point, the mist touches down on the leaves and flowers and forms a thin white layer of ice on the plants and the ground.

It's hard to find anything more beautiful than dew on flower petals and leaves. Clear, crystal-like dew is loved by the plants. A single drop of dew falls off the tip of a sprouting leaf on a branch and make its descent, through the forest canopy, and lands on the back of a frog. Thus, in the forest morning, water spreads itself about in multiple forms to shower love on the frog and the new sprout—and to be loved in return. Just as a mother instinctively loves her newborn, water in infancy is loved by all of nature.

After falling as rain or forming as dew onto the ground, what is water's next destination? Some water will be taken in by the roots of plants and then evaporate again into the atmosphere, but much more will seep slowly into the ground and begin an incredibly long leg of the total journey. Its main path will be the infinite number of secret tunnels under our feet.

The ground is filled with spaces of air, such as the tiny tunnels created by creatures out of our sight: earthworms, centipedes, spiders, beetles, bugs, mites, countless microorganisms, along with moles, rabbits, and other animals. All these creatures serve to soften the soil by opening spaces in the ground in every direction. Spaces between rocks and sand, and openings left by melted ice, rotted roots, dehydrated soil, and cracked stones, all serve as possible pathways for water on its incredible journey.

Water moves through layers of sand and clay and bedrock. Its journey downward is unwearied and profound. Depending on the hardness of the ground, it's not uncommon for water to move as little as 30 centimeters in a year's time.

Deep within the earth, when water finally reaches hard clay or bedrock, the droplets of water come together and flow into streams, sometimes becoming rivers or lakes such as those that exist above the ground and have names we know.

From the time when water left on this journey through the ground early in its infancy, it has gained experience and knowledge and has formed a personality depending on its path in life, much as a person's personality is formed by his or her journey. Water that has experienced coal, for example, has knowledge of calcium and magnesium, which is why we call it hard water. And water that has experienced granite is mostly left unchanged by minerals and is known as soft water.

Eventually, water learns all it can from the ground and is ready for the next stage in life. Out of darkness, it moves upward, toward the light above ground, and then after untold adventures and experiences, water emerges into the light.

From the ground's crevices rises water, cold and pure. From a tiny spring, water merges with other water fallen fresh from the sky and water permeating the soil to form a small stream that makes its way downward until, eventually, a river is born.

The river builds momentum and eats away at layers of soil and ground as the flow slowly widens and deepens, like a bright-eyed child emerging from infancy. The river becomes strong enough to carve away at a mountain or even to create a canyon. But the carving away of hard rocks and ground is not accomplished by water alone; most of this work is accomplished by the gravel and sand caught up in the flow of the water. These small particles carried along by water carve away at the surrounding land and bring in even larger rocks and stones, building enough strength to eventually carve away even the largest of stones.

The river begins to develop characteristics that give the river its reputation. While one river becomes dark brown from the earth it carries with it, another one flows clear and pure, and still another roars downward, smashing against rock and stone.

In its downward journey, water witnesses a great deal. It might witness salmon migrating upstream. Deer, bears, squirrels, and other creatures gather on its banks to quench their thirst. And trees brought down by a storm might even alter its flow.

The river eventually comes to gentler reaches, and now it flows gently as it winds along like an enormous snake crawling boldly across a plain. Never satisfied with its current course, the river will continue to change, at one point widening and letting sediment accumulating into a sand-bank, and then later narrowing to grind its way past stone.

If we could see the passage of ages in seconds, we would see just how much rivers turn and twist over time. Most rivers plot their courses so slowly that it defies human measurement, but there are some that shift relatively quickly. The Mississippi River, for example, has been known to shift by more than 20 meters in a single year.

After a river has shifted, the sand and soil it carries often accumulates and forms natural banks. Then a flood will come and wash away the bank, pushing the sediment onto the flat land. These floodplains become fertile land that gives birth to civilizations.

The Egyptian empire arose along the fertile floodplain of the Nile. So while floods are considered natural disasters, they also provide land with nourishment that civilizations require to establish themselves and grow.

When water encounters human beings, it has even more to witness. An old man crossing a bridge, a young girl on her bicycle, a couple sitting and watching the river flow. Ever slowly and ever gently, the river watches children playing in the park on its banks and a father and son playing catch.

The river, now in its twilight years, becomes ever more gentle as it inches toward the sea. Then the moment comes when it finally touches the sea, and the flowing of water finally comes to an end.

All the sediment carried by the water is then dropped into the estuary of the river. The result is the formation of a delta. The Ganges, the Mississippi, and the Amazon rivers have all formed great broom-like deltas at the points where they enter the ocean. What must have started as a small sandbank eventually grew into a great expanse of land, creating a new and spacious coastline. These fertile deltas form some of the greatest agricultural regions in the world—the final gift that water has to offer humankind before, at the end of its life, it gives itself up to the ocean.

But this is not really the end of life for water, for the ocean is also teeming with life, and together with all the creatures of the sea, water is even now just beginning. In the process of eternal rebirth, water is there to give us a full account of all its wisdom and experience. In a cycle that we would count as eternity, water travels the path from above the earth to the tips of mountains and to the depths of the ocean, carrying life within its bosom and linking everything together in perfect balance.

~~~~~~~

As water makes it journey through life, it becomes a witness to all of life on earth, becoming itself the flow of life.

For the second collection of water-crystal photographs in this book, we took photographs of water collected at various points along water's cycle, from the source to the bottom reaches of rivers. We also exposed water to various photographs of nature and plants to see how the water would reveal itself through crystals. Within the crystals can be seen the reflection of life.

Let Water Flow

Much of human history has been set along the banks of rivers. The great cultural hearths of civilization have all developed along the banks of rivers—the Nile, the Tigris and Euphrates, the Indus, and the Yellow River. And wherever explorers have traveled, they searched for water along their way.

From the days of the horse-drawn carriage to the automobile, rivers have observed the workings of our race. Today people continue to walk along the banks of rivers, talking with friends, looking at the flowing water, and speaking their hopes and dreams.

But now, armed with technology and knowledge, we work to change the very flow of water under the belief that the result will yield great benefits for humankind. And we have succeeded. Or so it would seem.

In 1971, construction on the Nile River of the Aswan High Dam, 3.6 kilometers across and 110 meters high, was completed. Its construction had required the relocation of the enormous and ancient Temple of Abu Simbel, along with 100,000 people who lived in the area. The completion was met with cheers of joy. Mankind had finally conquered the Nile, putting an end to a long history of flooding while also producing enough electricity for a quarter of Egypt's population.

But gradually it became clear what the river really had provided. After being dammed, the Nile was no longer capable of nourishing the once-fertile farmland at the delta. Irrigation systems were implemented, and for the first time chemical fertilizers were used. Irrigation raised the salt density and deteriorated the quality of the topsoil. Puddles and pools of water formed on the delta, becoming a breeding ground for harmful insects and causing great harm to nearby residents. The delta plain itself has even started to sink. Scientists soon noticed that the fish population in the dam was becoming infected with mercury as the water from the mountain valleys drained into the dam. Plant life buried by the dam became the perfect breeding ground for bacteria; as this bacteria absorbed the mercury in the ground, it became a highly toxic bacteria containing methylmercury. The density in the ecosystem steadily rose until it entered the bodies of fish in alarming amounts.

The annual flooding of the Nile may have made life along its shores difficult for humans, but it was an integral part of the life cycle for many other creatures. The dam squelched the vast ecosystem that nature had taken hundreds of thousands of years to form.

Similar effects are seen in other parts of the world when rivers are dammed. In Canada, high levels of mercury have been found in hair samples of the Cree Indians living around the James Bay and Peace River since the lake where they fished was dammed up to make a reservoir for generating electricity. This same phenomenon can be seen in other parts of Canada as well.

These are examples of what can happen when we choose to block or change the flow of water.

~~~~~~

The time has come for us to put on the brakes and think. Always keep in mind water's pure, natural journey, and you will see how we as humans fit into this delicate cycle of life. We are part of the flow, and we need to respect it. We have seen how water shows its love by showering its gifts onto flowers, trees, birds, insects, and all the small creatures of nature as it flows along its path. In return, water is loved by all of nature.

It's time that we return to the cycle. When you have learned to love nature from the bottom of your heart, then you too will be ready to be loved by nature.

The earth knows how to answer our most earnest prayers. When you pray, the earth responds. Then love spreads to all life and to water.

~~~~~~~~~~~~~~~~~~~

CHAPTER FOUR

The Wonder of Hado:
Explaining the Inexplicable

"**L**ong ago at the top of a distant mountain lived an old shaman . . ." So began a tale told to me by an old aborigine with a white scraggly mustache and a face darkened by time. He's in his late eighties, but no one, not even himself or his family, knows his exact age. Wisdom and knowledge accumulated over the decades is as deep as the wrinkles in his face.

I was on my first lecture trip to Australia in August 2002 when I was introduced to Eric, the aborigine elder. We met at a restaurant, and I presented him with a collection of my photographs of water crystals. He looked at it slowly and intently, and then he began to tell me an ancient tale passed down for generations.

This evil shaman lived at the top of Mount Ridge in the northern region now known as New South Wales. A river runs down the mountain, and the shaman lived near the upper reaches of the river.

One day she looked down on the river valley and saw all the happy people who lived along the banks of the river. The sight of all this happiness filled her heart with resentment, and she copied her thoughts into the water. She filled the river with spite and the desire that only she would be happy.

She also blocked up the river so only a trickle of water reached the people. The riverbed where pure water once freely ran became filled with filth. The people who lived along the banks of the river soon became sick, and thievery, bickering, and fighting became rampant because of the evil thoughts copied into the water by the shaman.

Years of pain and sorrow passed. Then one day a young shaman in the valley went for a walk with his dog. The dog chased after a kangaroo it saw, and the shaman waited for a long time for his dog to return. When the dog finally returned, he was dripping wet with pure water, not the foul water from the river.

Wanting to know where the pure water came from, the young shaman followed his dog up the mountain to the doorstep of the evil shaman's house. Nearby, the young shaman saw where the pure water of the river had been blocked.

The young shaman turned the evil shaman into water, and in a moment she was washed down by the river. They say that the rugged fissures at the far reaches of the river were caused by the evil shaman clawing at the edges, trying to save herself from being washed out to sea.

Just in time, she grabbed hold of a big rock. The young shaman spoke to her and said, 'I will save your life if you change your ways. Stay where you are now and promise to work for the good of people.'

The evil shaman promised to do so, and she became a large tree growing on top of the rock. The people along the riverbank were finally able to go back to living happy and peaceful lives. The old shaman, in the form of a tree, stood along the river to warn the people to stay away from the dangerous ledges.

Listening to Eric's story, I was surprised to hear the phrase "copied into the water." I then realized that this was in complete accordance with the principle of hado. I would never have imagined that this phrase would be found within a story handed down from generation to generation for thousands of years. But I should have realized that the more years one has lived, the more likely one is to know that such things are possible.

It was quite unexpected that I would hear such a story about water in such a distant corner of the world. Like the myths and fables of other countries and cultures, those of the aborigines in Australia are rich in truths about the universe and the ways in which life should be lived.

From the fable told by the elder, we learn that water must always flow. When the flow is stopped, then the river will die. We also learn that jealousy and greed have the power to destroy that which is good—an appropriate message for the times we live in.

Yet another lesson is that water has the ability to read emotions and to spread the hado of such emotions to the rest of the world. In other words, the messages that water carries throughout the world depends on each one of us, for better or worse.

For our ancestors, fantasy, science, and theology were all one and the same. And the way to pass on the truths of the world to future generations was through stories. Such stories were based on an understanding of the invisible laws that govern the visible world.

The advanced medical practitioners were the shamans who prayed for and healed the afflicted. Such is the role of water crystals. In fact, my journey toward water-crystal research was born out a desire to heal.

I was first introduced to the strange and wonderful world of hado more than fifteen years ago. I had just set up my company, IHM (originally International Health Medical, now International Hado Membership), and was importing a low-frequency medical device used to alleviate pain from the United States. My contact in the States was a biochemist named Dr. Lee H. Lorenzen. I learned that Dr. Lorenzen's wife had been quite ill. He had done all he could think of to restore her health, but nothing seemed to work. He finally decided to consider water.

He formed a team of scientists specializing in electronics and physics with the goal of developing the best water possible. They started their research with the proposition that water had the ability to transfer information. I heard from Dr. Lorenzen that they had actually found this water. Then one day I had the opportunity to see for myself what the water could do.

Under the bright blue skies of California, I was playing golf with Dr. Lorenzen and two of the researchers working with him when my left ankle started to ache from an old rugby injury. The other three noticed that I was limping and were concerned.

When we finally got back to the clubhouse, one of the men handed me a small plastic container with water in it. They instructed me to apply the water to the area around my ankle. I knew on one level that water couldn't remove pain, but I also knew that it couldn't hurt either, so I applied the water to my swollen ankle.

To my amazement, my foot no longer hurt when I walked on it, nor even when I stretched it out. I couldn't help but become interested in this strange water.

In Japan at that time, there was widespread interest in various types of water that claimed to be good for the health, so I signed a contract to introduce this technology to Japan, and I invited Dr. Lorenzen and the two researchers to seminars in three of the largest cities in the country.

At all three locations, perhaps because there was no charge to get in, the halls were overflowing with people. But I soon learned that the explanation of water's healing abilities was far too difficult for most people to grasp. I myself could hardly understand what the scientists were describing. Some people got up and left partway through; many others nodded off in their chairs. It was pretty much a disaster.

Afterward, I reflected on what went wrong. I realized that water is essential to human life in so many ways, and yet we really don't understand much about it. Around that time when I was still thinking about what to do next, I heard something that made sense to me: "Science is based on first forming a hypothesis and then using instruments and technology to prove the hypothesis."

Then it hit me. All sorts of instruments and technology can be used to analyze chemicals and other materials, so why isn't there anything that can be used to analyze water? I wasted no time in calling Dr. Lorenzen to ask him to look for a device of some type that we could use to analyze water. This led to my encounter with the MRA device that analyzes and transfers hado.

Since bringing this device to Japan in 1987, I have had the pleasure of working with as many as

15,000 people who have come to me with concerns about their health. I have written more than ten books about hado and the many miraculous cases I witnessed.

Over the years, scores of people have tried to imitate this hado machine and have made similar devices to analyze hado, creating a type of hado fad in Japan. Vast numbers of people have become interested in learning about the unseen world of hado. This movement has the energy to take us into a new age and open the door to a new stage of our evolution.

Understanding hado gives us a better under-standing of how our world works, and it also gives us hope for the future. I sometimes even think that knowing the possibilities of hado is like possessing a golden lamp that can make the impossible possi-ble. Then at other times, I feel that the more I understand hado, the more there is to understand about what's going on around us.

Photographing Crystals Is a Subjective Science
To gain the understanding and support of as many people as possible, I have approached my research as

scientifically as possible. But we can't forget that not everything can be understood by research or science. The photographs of water crystals present to us a majestic fantasy world, but this is a fantasy world that has much to teach us, for sometimes fantasy is the best way to get a clear picture of reality.

When water is frozen, the same crystal will never appear twice, just as there are no two snowflakes that are exactly alike. When I show slides of crystals at lectures, I am often asked, "If no two crystals are alike, how do you choose one particular crystal photograph?"

It's a good question. Of course it would be impossible to show you all the hundreds of photographs we take of all the crystals, but then again, I don't see why this should cause grave concern. It would be like looking at an encyclopedia of animals and questioning how the picture of one particular dog could possibly represent all the different dogs of that species. When I choose a photograph for a collection, I make a choice based on the photograph of the crystal that most accurately represents the crystals made under a certain set of circumstances.

In *The True Power of Water*, I briefly described how we photograph water crystals. I'd like to add more details to that explanation. If we are testing the effects on water of words, photographs, or music, we begin with distilled water and then expose the water to whatever influence we are testing for the appropriate amount of time. If we are testing water from a source such as a lake, we do not expose it to any outside influence, such as words or music. We simply use the water as is.

To photograph water crystals, we put 0.5 cc of water into about fifty petri dishes using a syringe. Then we freeze the petri dishes to minus 25 degrees centigrade and take photographs through a microscope. Of course, the result is never fifty similar crystals in the fifty petri dishes.

When we have the photographs, we divide them into eight categories: beautiful, rather beautiful, hexagonal pattern, radial pattern, lattice pattern, indefinite pattern, collapsed pattern, and no crystal formation.

This classification helps to give us a general idea of the type of crystals formed. Let's take, for example, the crystals made from water collected from the Honmyo River shown on pages 185–186. When we took water from the river before it runs into the Isahaya Bay in the Ariake Sea, we found that the crystals were broken and no complete hexagonal crystals formed. The results were as follows:

Beautiful: 0
Rather beautiful: 0
Hexagonal pattern: 0
Radial pattern: 2
Lattice pattern: 6
Indefinite pattern: 29
Collapsed pattern: 2
No crystal formation: 11

This shows us that no crystal formations appeared in eleven of the petri dishes, and when crystals did form they were broken. There was a not a single crystal that could be considered beautiful. Based on this, we then chose a crystal that we felt best represents the array of samples—an indefinite pattern, in this case.

Let's next look at the example of crystals formed from water collected near the source of the Honmyo River. The results were as follows:

Beautiful: 2
Rather beautiful: 4
Hexagonal pattern: 0
Radial pattern: 4
Lattice pattern: 8
Indefinite pattern: 29
Collapsed pattern: 3
No crystal formation: 0

In this case, we chose a beautiful crystal to represent the sample. Of course, there were only two beautiful crystals in the sample of fifty. But when such crystals appear from a sample, there are also usually many crystals that are classified as rather beautiful, hexagonal pattern, radial pattern, and lattice pattern. This indicates that there are many formations that are in the process or have the potential to make beautiful crystals.

Considering that crystals easily form from this particular sample of water, we can justifiably choose a beautiful crystal to represent the sample. I admit that the selection process is not strictly in accordance with the scientific method, but simply put, we choose the crystal that best represents the entire sample instead of simply one from the most common category.

And the whim of the person doing the selecting certainly comes into play. When making the selection for a collection of crystal photographs, it is best if one person chooses all the photographs for consistency, which is why all the photographs in this book were selected by me.

In fact, the crystals in the photographs that we take are affected by such factors as the environment, the timing, and even the personality and thoughts of the photographer. This is not unlike the uncertainty principle of quantum mechanics. The uncertainty principle was first put forth by a Germany physicist named Werner Heisenberg, and it is said to have completed the science of quantum mechanics. The theory says that each time you look at electrons, they move in a different way. In other terms, the very act of observing results in a differing movement of the electrons, making observation impossible.

The reason for this is that human observation requires light, and when electrons are exposed to light electrons, the electrons are disrupted, making their direction impossible to predict. This means that we know very little about what is going on in the world around us. When this theory was first presented to the scientific community, it apparently came as quite a shock.

The same principle applies to water. It changes its form completely depending on the person doing the observing. Water's reaction will differ depending on whether the heart of the observer is filled with appreciation or with anger, and this difference is reflected in the formation of the crystals.

Another factor that makes the observation of crystals even more difficult is that the form changes moment by moment for the two-minute life of the crystal. The crystal will look quite a bit different depending on when the shutter is pushed. Uncertainty truly is a factor in everything in our world.

The sun rises in the morning and sets in the evening. That is one thing we can count on. But if you consider the long history of the universe, this phenomenon is something that has continued for only a short time, and it's something that won't go on forever. After some five billion years, the sun will gradually expand and eventually consume the earth. And that too is just a part of the process that the sun which lights our world today is going through. What's a mere five billion years of earth time when talking about the forever time of the universe?

The methods employed to photograph water crystals might not pass everyone's definition of being scientific, and there is a degree of uncertainty involved. In fact, there is much about the world of hado that is murky and that cannot be explained by the black-and-white standards of statistical analysis.

But when you think about it, all any scientist can do anyway is lift up one small corner of the veil that covers the truth of this world and then try to express it with words that the general population can stretch their minds around.

Everything Emits Hado

Another question that I'm frequently asked is, "How could exposing water to a picture or words possibly result in crystals that are so different from each other?" Even I must admit that this is a difficult question to answer.

I first got the idea of exposing water to words and photographs before I even thought about taking photographs of water crystals. I was experimenting with the hado machine I mentioned previously. When people suffering from health problems came to my office for consultation, I would test and analyze their hado and recommend water as one treatment. The water would be infused with hado to counteract their illness. If they were too ill to leave their bed, I would print out the person's name and then test the hado from the name. Or I would test the hado of their photograph. The scores of instances where the ill person healed convinced me that even photographs have their own hado. (To read more about these cases, please refer to *The True Power of Water*.)

You might refer to this hado as something like a desire. There are people, but not many, who are able to detect the hado emitted by photographs and thus are able to sense if a missing person is dead or alive from a photograph in the newspaper. Even people who would never admit to believing in such special powers may experience having a premonition and then later learn that their premonition was valid. An acquaintance of mine said he remembered reading about a mountain climber who had reached the top of Mount Everest. When he looked at the picture of the climber, he sensed that the climber was no longer alive. Not long after, he heard on the news that that the climber was lost and presumed dead. It's hard to deny that somewhere buried deeply within the human consciousness, there is a hidden power—perhaps intuition—to sense what has happened despite the barriers of time and distance.

This same thing can also be said of words. There's an ancient belief in Japan that each individual word has its own spirit, which makes it possible for messages to be transferred and information relayed.

When water is exposed to words such as "Thank you" and "You idiot!" we can see that the water accurately captures the characteristics of these words. But when words are spoken to water, the meaning of the words changes significantly with the speaker's intonation and inflection. The words "You idiot!" can have completely different meanings depending on whether they're said with deep-felt hatred or in jest. But with words written on paper, the way the word is said is not a factor, and the pure energy of the word is able to reveal itself in the formation of the crystal.

No matter how often or how deeply you consider it, it remains remarkable—almost unbelievable—that the messages of water are able to pass through the barriers of time and space.

The fact that a photograph contains information indicates that consciousness is involved. When you see a photograph of a landscape and think it's beautiful, or a picture of a friend that brings back old memories, the photograph is appealing to your consciousness. In the same way, an ID photo serves as ID because of the awareness that the picture represents the actual person.

A psychology professor at Yale University conducted an experiment a while back. He chose several words from Hebrew, and then he simply made up an equal number of words. Next he mixed all the words together, showed them to subjects who didn't know Hebrew, and had them guess the meanings of the words. The subjects, of course, did not know that half of the words were fake. The result was that there were significantly more right guesses for the Hebrew words than for the made-up words.

This experiment serves as support for the theories of Dr. Rupert Sheldrake, a scientist who believes that the words which people have used for ages form "morphic fields" for perception of the meaning of such words. So someone who has never seen a word can guess its meaning with an unexpected degree of accuracy. The morphic field is not anything you can see with the eyes, and it's not an energy that can be measured. It might best be described as another world invisible to the eye.

With the formation of a morphic field, there's an increased likelihood that something which happens twice will happen again. This same process can be seen in the unfolding of history. The words that have already been spoken somewhere in the world are somehow easier to learn.

To illustrate this idea, let's look at an example. On a visit to Germany a while back, I heard an amazing story. A doctor had collected blood samples from several patients and stored them. The doctor said he was able to identify what the patient was ailing from by just looking at his or her blood sample.

The samples were sealed and stored to keep them from being contaminated or altered. But two years later, when the physician reexamined the patients and the previous samples, he noticed that the components of the blood had changed, and not just randomly. The two-year-old blood was now changed to the same components as the recently reexamined blood. In other words, if a patient was sick two years previously and then healthy after, the two-year-old blood changed to be that of a healthy person, and vice versa. The doctor then went on to conduct two thousand more experiments and to publish the results.

I met another doctor, a man in his eighties, in Germany who had conducted a similar experiment. He had used a pendulum to conduct diagnoses by taking a drop of blood from the patient's finger and soaking it into a piece of paper. He said that he could use the same bloodstain throughout the treatment of the patient, because it continued to change in appearance according to the patient's condition. In other words, a bloodstain from two years ago could be used to diagnose the current condition of the patient.

The scientific explanation for this? I do not know.

How can we interpret the principles of hado? Think about the three terms we discussed in the first chapter of this book concerning hado.

First, hado is vibration. All human beings are in a state of vibration, and the condition of an individual can be understood by examining the vibration of a blood sample from that person.

Second, hado is resonance. Blood taken from a person two years ago remains in resonance with the person's hado today, changing to match the current status of the blood flowing through the veins now.

And third, hado is similarity. For all hado, there is a miniature and a macro version, and these versions resonate with each other. In the experiments done in Germany, my interpretation is that the blood sample is a miniature version of the sample's body, changing in unison with the body from whence it came.

About seven decades ago, a scientist named Harold Saxton Burr laid much of the basic foundation for the science of hado. Burr was a renowned professor of anatomy at Yale University. In his attempt to understand the mysteries of life, he gave us the term *L-field* or *life field*. Since all the cells within our bodies are replaced over a period of six months, why do we keep being reborn as the same person over and over?

Like a mold used to make Jell-O, an invisible force enables this to happen, he believed, and he called it the "life field." He believed that since the life field is an electrical field in nature, it could be measured, and he even developed his own measuring device using a voltage indicator and an electrode. He discovered that the measurements he took varied with the way the subject was feeling. He got higher voltage readings from subjects who were feeling blissful, and lower voltage readings from those feeling depressed.

It seems that his device was a forerunner for the MRA device that I use to analyze hado. By entering various code numbers into the device, it's possible to identify the part of the body that matches the code. When a certain part of your body is suffering, emotional hado is inevitably involved. By using the codes, such emotional hado can also be measured and classified.

In his book *Blueprint for Immortality: The Electric Patterns of Life*, Dr. Burr wrote that someday it will be possible to pinpoint even the emotions of people using millivolts.

Anyone who has worked very much with vibration has noticed at least one thing: the soul is affected by anything, and it *affects* everything. Both your body and the things that go on around you—and even the world that you live in—is created by your soul. It's something that I have observed over and over. There is so much power within you.

Perhaps we do live in a world of uncontrollable and unpredictable chaos. We really don't know what's going to happen from one moment to the next.

But this chaos is also of your own creation. Chaos is brimming over with myriad amounts of energy. After all, before heaven and earth, before there was a universe moving in order, there was just one thing: chaos.

So if you feel lost, disappointed, hesitant, or weak, return to yourself, to who you are, here and now.

And when you get there, you will discover yourself, like a lotus flower in full bloom, even in a muddy pond, beautiful and strong.

~~~~~~~~~~

CHAPTER FIVE

Our World and Our Water
Are Changed by Prayer

When I was a child, I had a recurring nightmare. The ground shook beneath my feet, and a volcano spewed out red-hot lava. The ocean turned into a huge wave that enveloped everything, knocking over houses and buildings like blocks, and all the people ran about screaming as the earth moaned.

There was a time when it seemed like I had this dream every night. I'm no longer bothered by the dream. In fact, it stopped when I published my first book of water crystals. But I suspect I have seen

143

the dream thousands of times over the years. Sometimes it scared me so much that I jumped out of bed wide awake and ready to run for my life. To this day, I still don't know the meaning of the dream or why I saw it over and over. I know it was just a dream, but that scene of hell still lurks in my memory as if it were real.

The turn of the century seemed to be a time of particular uncertainty and instability. One of the outcomes was a greater interest in spiritual matters. Yes, we survived July 1999, the month when Nostradamus said the world would be destroyed, and 2000 came and went without all our computers turning against us. While many people can recall a feeling that something dreadful was about to happen, many others believed that we stood at the brink of a period in human history when all the knowledge and wisdom of the ages just might culminate to create a golden age. And those who didn't have such a feeling at least hoped for such a future. But the hopefulness wasn't to last long.

September 11, 2001, came and nothing was the same. The flames of war ignited in the Middle East, Afghanistan, Iraq, and Israel. The first page of our new hope-filled century was stained with blood. Then came the devastating Indian Ocean tsunami in December 2004 and Hurricane Katrina in 2005. And I recalled the nightmare of my childhood.

There have always been people who believe the end of the human race, the destruction of the world, and global catastrophe are imminent. I don't believe such a bleak future is waiting for us, and I've always tried to take a stand against such negative predictions. The reason for my optimism is that I feel that the words engraved in our hearts might just have an effect on the direction in which the world is moving.

But I must admit that it sometimes does seem that the world is taking the steps which will lead straight to the destruction of the human race. No matter how positive you try to be, it's hard to ignore the fact that we are faced by an avalanche of problems of our own creation.

With the global population expected to explode by 1.5 times in the next fifty years and four times in the next one hundred years, with rapid industrialization, with the condition of the environment deteriorating at a rapid pace, our survival is uncertain.

Some reports say that a temperature increase of between 4 and 6 degrees centigrade within one hundred years will increase the ocean level by 80 to 150 centimeters and flood much of the land we currently inhabit.

And there's no guarantee that the change will be gradual. Large islands in the South Seas are already now slipping into the ocean. The rising of the oceans combined with a tsunami similar to the one we just witnessed could wipe out many of the great cities and entire civilizations in some parts of the world. Instable weather patterns are another concern. Unusual downpours and droughts are wreaking havoc with the world's food supply.

I sometimes wonder if the recurring dream I saw a child wasn't more than just a child's dream. What could we possibly do to change this course even slightly? One solution is to change the way we live and the structures and systems that form society.

Environmental Concerns

In chapter 3, I discussed the destructive repercussions of blocking the flow of water. We see the same results when we interfere with the delicate circle of life that forms ecosystems.

One of the first warning bells was the book *Silent Spring* by Rachel Carson, who revealed that pesticides such as DDT pollute the water and push entire species of birds and fish to the brink of extinction. *Silent Spring* told the story of how the insecticide dieldrin was sprayed in and around Sheldon, Illinois, in order to eradicate the Japanese beetle in that area and stop its northern progression. The chemicals seeped into the ground, killing or driving out all the beetles and other insects. After eating the insects or bathing in the polluted water, the death of robins, pheasants, and starlings came next, followed by the deaths of squirrels, rabbits, and then 90 percent of farm cats. Even sheep could not escape the fatal effects of the chemicals.

Carson also revealed the impact of the chemicals on the salmon and trout in rivers, and the rising cancer rate in humans. But all this didn't stop the state and federal governments from spraying stronger and stronger insecticides for years to come.

As expected, her work earned protests from the agrichemical industry. They made fun of the book and labeled her a hysterical woman. But when Carson appeared in the press to defend herself, her logic and her dignity made and even deeper impression on the viewers. Eventually this led to the government being forced to admit that she was right. Carson's good judgment and courage reaches beyond her time and has just as much to teach us today. Her book should be required reading for anyone living in these times.

Carson sounded an early warning about the potential risks of pollution, but she also warned us about the chain effect that results when a link of the circle of life is broken. We have already seen where the removal of bugs or weeds by chemical means can lead to the extinction of a vast area of other forms of life, including the microorganisms that live in the soil. And when the soil has died, then the perpetual use of chemicals becomes necessary to continue farming.

Once the natural circle of life is broken, putting it back together is next to impossible. Some forty years have passed since Rachel Carson first warned us about the effects of pesticides. Have we seen any improvement in the situation? In advanced countries, at least, the use of DDT, dieldrin, and other chemicals that Carson warned us about have been banned and for the most part discontinued. But deplorably, these chemicals are still sold to other countries that haven't banned them yet.

In our pursuit for profit and convenience, we have closed our eyes to the cycle of life that has formed over the aeons. So much of what we do threatens to end this cycle and create a new cycle of waste and destruction.

Ever-Increasing Materialism

Do you ever get the feeling that society in general and you in specific are moving at a faster pace than ten or twenty years ago? It's not likely that the hands of our clocks have sped up, but our perception of time certainly has.

Imagine that the world is an enormous spinning top. We'll call it the "top of materialistic culture." As culture develops and we acquire more and more, the top gets bigger and bigger. This is how life goes in our materialistic state. Each year, sales have to increase, incomes have to rise, and economies have to expand. We're made to think that staying the same or slowing down will lead to recession, depression, and failure. Goals achieved lead to the setting of higher goals and requirements to work ever harder and faster. Ever loyal, we have labored diligently to expand the size of the spinning top.

And we at the edge of this top must travel an increasingly wider distance to make one rotation. While a small top might complete a rotation in one second, a top twice as large—or a thousand times larger—would take much longer to go around once. While a small top may rotate a few centimeters per second, a larger top may travel a few meters.

The speed of the hands on your clock are going at the same speed, but the rate at which change takes place is speeding up, and perhaps someday this spinning top will go so fast that we'll no longer be able to hang on. How can we slow down this spinning top?

I know of only one way, and that is to cast aside our fast-paced, materialistic lifestyles. In other words, our continued sojourn on this planet will require that we pack lighter. It's just that simple.

You may believe that you can get more accomplished in less time if you live your life in overdrive, but for most people it ends up meaning working harder and harder in a job they like less and less.

As society expands and infrastructures become more complicated, the role of the individual is increasingly delegated to a miniscule piece of a vast machine; feeling powerless to make a difference, people resign themselves to doing what they are told to do and nothing more. But the greatest steps forward can often be made by becoming smaller instead of bigger, by going slower instead of faster.

Within an organization, workers are able to expand their abilities only to the limits of the box within which they function. In many large companies with compartmentalized divisions, the scope of most people is limited to the task at hand. With only a small role to perform within a large box, the importance and value of each role is minimal, as is the employee's perspective and need to develop his or her abilities. But when the size of the box that people function within is reduced, the role of the people within the box becomes more important and valuable, and knowing this, most people will strive to expand their skills and abilities. They get to know their co-workers, communication improves, and motivation increases. Ideas that were formerly obscured by the complexities of the big organization would emerge and innovations would revolutionize the organization. Young employees in the company would see hope and be motivated by their unlimited potential to move up in the company. The concept that smaller is better applies not only to companies. These same results could be seen in governments and all other organizations in society.

A Changing Sentiment

More and more people are beginning to understand that bigger and faster is not necessarily better. It is becoming clearer that continually piling unreasonable greed and demand on top of each other leads to destruction rather than success. It's not unusual to see financial institutions, construction companies, and retailers fighting for their survival. We might even say that the destruction of the World Trade

Center was symbolic of a broader change taking place in our society. Of course the terrorist attacks were a heinous crime, but one reason the twin towers in New York were targeted by the terrorists was because they were a symbol of the global economy and one of the most enormous building complexes ever built. I believe that its collapse has played a role in moving us humans toward the theory of E. F. Schumacher, who advocates "Small is beautiful" in his new economics with humans in its center.

Many people today are coming together to form communities beyond the typical definitions of neighborhood and village. In Europe, the United States, Australia, and other parts of the world, communities are forming with the aim of living peacefully with the environment. These communities take various forms, but they all have the basic goal of separating themselves from consumer-based lifestyles and becoming self-sufficient. Another aspect of this trend is the slow-food movement and the rising voice against the drive for standardization promoted by globalism.

In recent years, we've also heard talk of new regional currencies and the drive to implement systems that return to focusing on the exchange of goods and labor of equal value instead of the continual expansion of speculation that is going on now. This is another way that we are returning to the fundamentals of the concept of community.

A Natural, Renewable Alternative to Oil

One thing that these new old concepts of community have in common is concern for the environment. For a long time, oil has been a source of major concern and conflict for the world. Most world economies are powered by oil, as are many of the wars going on in the world. And that's to be expected. Energy is at the foundation of all cultures. We owe our comfortable lifestyles to our ability to procure sufficient amounts of it. We can keep the neon lights on all night. There's always a store open nearby to feed our hunger and our desire of the moment.

But what will happen to us when the last drop of oil is used up? The lights will go out and our appliances will be useless. But it won't matter because we won't be able to transport food to our tables. The foundation supporting us is frail indeed.

If it's not cramping our style today, then we tend to think it's a problem for someone else. But now in times of abundance is when we should be laying the foundation for the survival of future generations. We need to be looking for something to replace oil and the oil-based products that we so rely on.

One possible alternative that has caught my attention is hemp. Nature provides for us in many wonderful ways, so we should look to nature first for solutions to our challenges. The hemp plant can provide many of the things that humankind requires in order to survive on this planet.

From its stalk, paper, cloth, and even plastic can be produced. Four times more paper can be made from an acre of hemp than from an acre of trees. The cloth made from hemp is much more gentle on the skin than chemical-soaked cotton, not to mention that hemp is three to four times more efficient than cotton as a crop.

From the seed and stalk of the hemp, diesel fuel, methanol, and ethanol can be obtained without the by-products of sulfur that causes acid rain and air pollution. Ford Motors has even made a car with a plastic body made from hemp that runs on hemp fuel.

Hemp can also become an ideal source of human nourishment. The fruit of the hemp plant provides the same amount of protein found in soybeans, and it is easy to digest. It also contains essential amino and fatty acids.

The hemp seeds can also be used to make a healthy oil. *Huo Ma Ren* is the Chinese name for it, and it is widely used as herbal medicine. Its medical uses are numerous. Possible derivative products include an antibiotic, antidepressant agent, pain reliever, and headache medicine. It's also reported to have shown dramatic results in the treatment of cancer, AIDS, rheumatism, and skin rashes. Hemp can also be used to make shampoos and cosmetics because of its moisturizing characteristics.

Another feature that makes hemp attractive is its rapid growth rate. In 110 days, the plant will reach a height of two or three meters, making it possible to harvest several crops in a single season. In Japan, it's said that ninja would use hemp to improve their jumping skills. When the plant first started to grow, they could easily jump over the top of it, but as it grew taller day by day, it required more and more effort and skill to clear.

As the hemp plant grows, it converts carbon dioxide into oxygen at a faster rate than almost any other plant. The amount of carbon dioxide taken in by hemp is pound for pound three to four times more efficient than deciduous leaves.

From a hado perspective, hemp is good for the environment because it has positive hado. In fact, hemp's high rate of vibration is what enables it to grow so quickly. It is a gift of nature that could come to our rescue just when we need it.

Hemp is woven into the fabric of America's history. It's said that without hemp to make ropes and sails, Columbus would have never been able to make the trip across the ocean. Even the Declaration of Independence is written on hemp paper. You could even find hemp growing on George Washington's farm.

Unfortunately, there are misconceptions about hemp because of its relation to marijuana, or cannabis, which is illegal in many parts of the world. Despite this, there has been a grassroots reawakening in recent years to the potential uses of hemp. In July 2001, the Hemp Car, a biodiesel car running on fuel from the seed of the hemp plant, left Washington D.C. and started on a trip across America to promote the benefits of hemp as a resource. The efforts to attract attention to this amazing new source of fuel were going well until the news was buried by the events of September 11.

In Japan as well, a hemp car also crossed the country in 2002. A man named Yasunao Nakayama has made it his life's calling to promote the use of hemp. He says that he sees hemp as essential for the survival of the human race.

As a teenager, Nakayama-san came close to drowning and had a near-death experience. The young man found himself surrounded by light in another world where people were going about their lives. He saw a plant with beautiful leaves and recognized a wonderful sense of healing coming from the plant. When he came to, the experience made him think in a deep way about the purpose of life.

Several years had passed when Nakayama-san encountered the plant that he had seen in his out-of-body experience. There was no doubt in his mind that this was the plant which would help him understand the mysteries of life and the universe. The plant of course was hemp, and since that time, Nakayama-san has made the study of hemp his life's work.

Japan's version of the hemp car left a small city in the northern tip of Japan with its destination the Heitate Shinto shrine in Kumamoto prefecture. In place of gas in the diesel engine, hemp oil was used. This biodiesel fuel emits no sulfur dioxide and only one-third the amount of toxic smog emitted by petroleum fuel.

During his journey, Nakayama-san visited many places related to hemp, including the hemp road of Japan that served as the network tying together an ancient self-sustaining society. In ancient days in Japan, many trade routes linked the country. Along with routes for salt, sugar, silk, and other products, there were also routes for transporting hemp. If you drive the hemp road you can see the traces that ancient Japan had an abundant self-sustaining society, which was based on a solar worship.

The Shinto Religion and Hemp

On its long journey through Japan, the hemp car made stops at the many Shinto shrines in Japan where hemp is considered to have special significance. Their ultimate destination, the Heitate Shrine, is considered the oldest shrine in Japan; even its name comes from the ancient Japanese word for hemp.

From ancient times, hemp played an important role in Shinto beliefs and practices. It was considered to have many powers, including the power to purify and cast out evil spirits. I suspect that one reason the ancients revered cannabis so much was its rapid rate of growth, indicating a high vibration rate. This enabled it to drive out evil, impurity, and other forms of low vibration.

Hemp's many uses in the temples include the braided ropes around sacred trees and the bell rope used to wake the gods at the entrance of the shrine. At the Ise Temple, the most sacred of all Shinto shrines, ancient cannabis is preserved along with the sacred mirror, serving as emblems of the body of Amaterasu, the founding Goddess of Japan. A sacred Amaterasu talisman is referred to as the shrine cannabis, and each year ceremonies take place according to the sacred "cannabis calendar."

The ancient Shinto religion of Japan can be described as a religion of vibration. It has no founder, no teachings, no sacred writings, and no ceremonies or practices with the aim of causing an awakening or rebirth. Shintoism is mostly about raising the vibration rate to drive out negative forces, thus creating holy spaces. It is said that the sites for ancient temples were chosen in areas of pristine nature that emitted a high energy level.

Shinto does not claim one founder or one god. Mountains, rivers, oceans, animals, trees, and flowers are all gods, and along with people, all elements of a single, unified universe. The soul of Shintoism is harmony. In nature, nothing is inferior and nothing is superior. All things are given a role and responsibility, and one part of the universe serves all other parts by best being who and what it is.

Perhaps the bountiful and beautiful nature of Japan had something to do with the emergence of such a concept. With the beauty, colors, sounds, and scents of four distinct seasons, the Japanese have become sensitive to the nature around them, making it possible to see multiple gods within nature and leading to the formation of a culture that promotes the richness and sacredness of vibration.

When Prayer Touches Water

The Shinto prayers referred to as *norito* are for the purpose of creating vibration, which will link us to the sacred. I have previously written that the hado from a certain type of voice can have the effect of prayer in healing. I have had many experiences with praying over water with the locals in places such as Lake Biwa (the largest lake in Japan); in Lucerne, Switzerland; on the shores of Lake Zurich; in the Bahamas; and in other parts of the world. In every case, there was a striking difference in the crystals made from water collected before the prayer and after the prayer, and the subsequent crystals were always beautiful and glorious.

Words spoken from a heart filled with prayer takes on the form of hado, and this leads to a new world being eternally created. Your world becomes different when things are created in a whole new way. The Shinto prayer is not a prayer to the One and Only but a prayer to myriad holy beings. What could we mean by myriad holy beings? From the perspective of hado, it is possible to form an idea.

Consider the fact that there are some sounds that can be perceived by the human ear and others that cannot. The highest sound that humans can hear is about 20 kilohertz, but there are certainly sounds that exist in a higher range than that, and we refer to this sound level as ultrasound. The same concept can be applied to light. The light spectrum visible to the human eye has an electromagnetic wave of between 380 and 780 nanometers, and anything outside of this range cannot be seen. But electromagnetic waves above 780 nanometers do exist.

This principle applies to all our senses—or perhaps we should say that what we can feel with our senses is only a small part of our world. The blind bat uses ultrasound that the human ear cannot hear to avoid hitting cave walls. A dog can distinguish between scents that are beyond our detection. Many animals have almost supernatural abilities.

Considering these facts, it would not be too much of a stretch of the mind to say that there are types of consciousness and life forms that are beyond our limited ability to sense. Perhaps it would not be so strange to believe in the existence of higher-frequency consciousness without a physical body like ours. If there is such a being, I suspect that it may exist in a parallel universe with our own world.

When a vibration is doubled, it is possible to create a new set of sounds one octave higher. And with each case of doubling, the octave goes higher and higher until we reach a set of sounds too high for the human ear to hear.

In the same way, rocks, grass, animals, and people all vibrate at their own rate and in octaves we are in tune with, and so it shouldn't be too difficult to surmise the existence of an equivalent frequency in octaves that are off our own scale of sensitivities. Within this line of theory, perhaps we can then come up with a description of the gods of all of creation. Perhaps we can form a link between ourselves and a higher being. The method I speak of is, of course, prayer.

Our Common Consciousness

No one I personally know has seen the face of a deity, although I realize there are people who say they have had this experience. All we can do is gather evidence and consider it. By considering it based on the principles of hado, I believe considerable progress is possible in this realm.

If you examine any culture—ancient or modern—you'll find that everyone has somehow arrived at a concept of deity. Genetic engineers, physicists, and other scientists who have reached to the edges of their fields become enraptured by the magnificence and order of nature and thus become convinced of some unseen hand at work in the creation. My own path to this understanding was shown to me by water crystals. Water has shown me in a very real way how prayer can change the world.

No one particular religion has been able to secure the exclusive rights for the power of prayer. No matter who we are, we all have the ability to take advantage of this amazing and wonderful power. Once you realize this, you will then be filled with the desire to help others realize this as well. More and more people are resonating with this understanding, and this could result in a more wonderful future for humankind.

In my presentations, I mention that I have another interpretation of Einstein's theory of relativity represented by the formula $E = mc^2$: c represents consciousness; m represents mass (the number of people); and when the number of people with an awakened consciousness founded in the desire to make the world a better place increases, the result is an exponential increase in E, or energy.

Earlier in this book, I talked about Professor Hideo Higa, who developed the unique microorganism EM. He explained to me that within the world of microorganisms, 10 percent of microorganisms are harmful. But there are also only 10 percent of beneficial microorganisms. He refers to the remaining 80 percent as wait-and-see microorganisms. They watch until either the good or the bad microorganisms emerge as the victors, and then they join the stronger of the two.

I find that there is a correlation to what goes on in human society. Within our society, there are people, about 10 percent, who have the ability and feel the call to make this world a better place. But many of these people have not yet become aware of their destiny. I am quite sure that as more and more of these people awaken and begin to employ their consciousness in prayer and action, the vast majority of the population—about 80 percent—will then also join their numbers.

The Water within Us

We are well into the twenty-first century, and blood continues to be shed. Especially painful to watch is the conflict between Palestine and Israel. How much life will have to be destroyed by ethnic fighting and holy war? Without an end to this horrendous conflict, it is hard to imagine a peaceful future for any of us. But it appears as if the hatred and loathing has over centuries slowly entered the very DNA of the two sides.

I was once thinking about this when I suddenly realized the close relationship between DNA and water. DNA is structured by two chains in a spiral formed by a hydrogen bond. The consciousness of our ancestors is passed from one generation to the next through blood—the *water* that circulates throughout our bodies. And the water that flows through the bodies of the Jews and Palestinians comes mostly from the Jordan River. The Jordan River flows southward from northern Palestine and connects the Sea of Galilee with the Dead Sea, forming the eastern border of Palestine. Along its way, it provides much of the water necessary for sustaining life in the region.

The power of prayer has the ability to reach far distances of space and time. Through the photographs of water crystals, I have strived to help people from around the world understand the power and wonder of prayer, and I have encouraged people everywhere to pray for peace in the world. I decided that I would ask people to join together on a particular day to send hado of love and peace to the Sea of Galilee, which flows into the Jordan River. The people who drink its water would receive this hado, and their bodies would be filled with beautiful energy. Can you just imagine the possibilities for peace?

Before I set the date, I discovered something quite surprising. Another name for the Sea of Galilee is Lake Kinneret, and *kinneret*, in Hebrew, is the word for *harp*—the shape of the Sea of Galilee. And it also happens that Lake Biwa is named after the *biwa*, a traditional harp-like instrument in Japan. Could the similarity be more than a coincidence?

I decided to set the day for the special prayer for July 25, 2003. As I mentioned in chapter 2, this day is very important on the thirteen-month calendar used by the Mayans. It is called "the day out of time," the one extra day on the Mayan calendar.

Even in this modern age, perhaps we have the spirit of this day buried within us. I intend to work toward making this an international day of prayer for expressing love and appreciation for water.

A year prior to the date I set for sending hado to the Sea of Galilee, I established what I call the Project of Love and Thanks to Water. This was a project aimed at unifying the souls of people from around the world and raising consciousness on July 25, 2003.

My first efforts focused on expanding the circle of people willing to participate in the prayer. I asked everyone I knew to do the following: On the 25th of each month, either at 7:25 in the morning or 7:25 in the evening, face a body of water and express your love and appreciation. You could do this anywhere, such as your kitchen or your bedroom. A glass of water would suffice. Gently say to the water, "I love you" and "Thank you." As you do this, imagine the power of love and appreciation flowing through you into all of the water of the world.

All water, even the glass of water, is connected to all the rest of the water in the rest of the world. The hado of love and appreciation that you release will become streams of brilliant gold and silver light in the flowing water and reach out to the entire world, ultimately covering it in light. The result will be a testimony of the healing and harmonizing of our planet.

Water carries within it your thoughts and your prayers. And as you yourself are water, no matter where you are, your prayers will be carried to the rest of the world.

So, pray. Pray for the victims of meaningless wars and landmines, for orphaned children, for the sick and the bedridden. There is much you can do from now on, and even a lot you can do at this very moment.

I recall that horrible recurring dream I saw as a small child. It wasn't warning me about my fate to witness the gloom and doom of the human race. It was teaching me what I must do in life. But it wasn't a lesson for me alone. It was for you and for everyone else who reads this book: Fill your soul with love and gratitude. Pray for the world. Share the message of love. And let us flow as long as we live.

~~~~~~~~~~~~~~~~~~

We are now approaching the end of this journey of water together. What discoveries did you make along the way? Water has a secret life. It shows us how to find happiness. It reveals the meaning of the love of nature. It shows us the path that humankind must take to find the answers we seek.

Water Is Life

James Lovelock, a professor of biophysics, put forth the Gaia Theory, the concept that the world is all one life form, an active self-regulating system. The environment on the earth is kept at a certain level so as to make life possible. The volume of oxygen in the atmosphere is always about 20 percent no matter where you go. Plant life produces oxygen through photosynthesis, and animals breathe out carbon dioxide. The atmosphere works to maintain the temperature within a set range. So even though the seasons may change, we manage to keep our body temperature fairly constant. They say that 3.5 million years have passed since the birth of life, and while the sun may be gradually heating up, the temperature on earth has been maintained within a range to make life possible. The world operates in perfect balance

Indeed, this planet is like one life form. And what is it that gives life to this living planet? Water, of course. Water makes it possible for plants to grow, to produce oxygen, and to maintain life. But we all realize that this balance of life is now becoming ever more perilous. We are even playing with the balance of the atmosphere.

Water Is Beauty

Water's long journey began when it arrived on this planet in the form of lumps of ice from the far reaches of the universe. From there arose all the diverse forms of nature and life that now cover the surface of this planet. And from that point, human civilization arose, and the life of each individual was born.

From water emanates all beauty: the colorful grandeur of nature, the green meadows, the silk strings of rain, the clouds that filter golden sunshine, the rainbow-filled skies, and the expansive sea, blue in gradation the deeper you go. Rays from the sun dance on the surface, reflecting off ocean plants and coral below. Fish of every color swim in schools that expand and contract again as if by magic. It is art, a grand performance, at its finest.

And then there's the crystals of water. Like pearls of the highest grade, finely carved by nature—almost like grand chandeliers.

The work of nature is far beyond the aspirations of the greatest artists. And the amazing thing is that it's no accident. It's all the result of a distinct intention, a hidden master plan. Its creation requires a level of intent and determination that we are incapable of understanding, much less mimicking.

So then, we must ask, who? Kazuo Murakami, professor emeritus at Tsukuba University in Japan, has used the term "something great." It is an existence that has put its signature on each one of the some sixty trillion cells of our bodies, each containing enough genetic information to fill thousands of books thousands of pages long. It is this "something great" that has brought order to the universe and that keeps it moving in order.

It was through such a consciousness that water was brought to this earth. It was brought to this earth for the creation of beauty.

Water Is a Mirror

Water reflects the human soul. If you say "Thank you" to water, it will be reflected in the formation of beautiful crystals overflowing with gratitude in return. If the hearts of those who live on the planet are contaminated, then the earth as well will become that way.

Very little pure water—only 3 percent of our total water—remains on the earth, and the amount suitable for human use is declining at alarming rates. Of all the water on the earth, the amount that falls from the skies and runs into the oceans is incredibly small. Almost all the water on earth is saltwater in the oceans, while most of the drinkable water is frozen in glaciers at the top of the tallest mountains. Compared to all the water that runs into the oceans, the amount available for our use is a tiny fraction, about 1/10,000th of all the water on the earth.

The outlook of the human race could be perceived as becoming more and more gloomy. The population is rising at a rapid rate, and even the groundwater, the source of last resort, is now becoming polluted. The pollution of water is the pollution of our very soul, and unless we change our consciousness, we will never be able to restore water to its pristine form.

Water Is Prayer

Water comes to earth as the answer to our prayers, and that process continues even now. What prayer, you ask? The prayer that life will be born, breathe, and take root. The prayer that nature will prosper, expand, and cradle what the native people call the "circle of life." The prayer that intelligence will emerge and civilizations will form to protect the earth and spread love and gratitude.

Why do you think it is that when water is shown the words "love and gratitude" such spectacular crystals form? The answer is that words are a form of prayer. When something is in line with the principles of nature and it interacts with water, the result is the formation of beautiful crystals. This is because nature itself is the result of prayer. Prayer is also the true nature of human beings. All races of people over time have had the element of prayer. Even in these present days when science reigns supreme, we still pray. What heart doesn't pray when a sick child clutches to life or when a loved one is far away?

Water is given to answer our prayer for life, for evolution, and so human beings can look toward water and offer their prayers. Human beings are essentially crystals formed upon this earth. And that is why we have the responsibility to protect the earth by protecting our water. And the first step we can take is to return prayer to our lives. I offer you a poem about water:

You are water and the wisdom of water
      you know.
So just allow yourself to flow,
And then the wonder grows . . .

Your soul will reach beyond the seas,
With harmony on prayers of peace . . .

Never stopping, never halting, bravely water flows . . .

Brightly and boldly into the cosmos, for water knows.

Springwater and dam water

We journeyed down the Kumano River to collect water samples along the cycle of water. At the southernmost tip of Honshu Island in Japan, the Kii Peninsula and Kumano Mountains protrude out into the ocean. From this land where nature gods are said to live in Japanese lore, we collected water and from it produced crystals.

Dew on a low, striped bamboo on a mountain trail

Springwater at the foot of a mountain

Water flowing into a river

We began our journey from an altitude of 1,800 meters and collected water from a low, striped bamboo leaf. Such droplets eventually spring from the ground and form streams that lead to rivers.

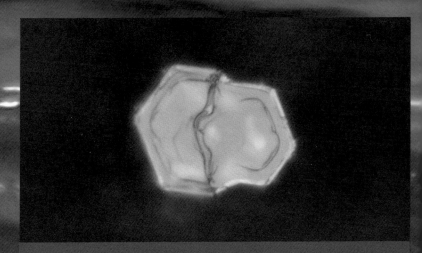

Dam water

A stream merging with a river

One kilometer downstream
from the dam

The crystals formed from the dam water lack any momentum. However, a
kilometer away from the dam, beautiful crystals are once again possible.
The stream eventually merges with the main river.

A flowing river and blocked-off water

At the edge of the Ariake Sea where the Honmyo River empties into Isahaya Bay, a land-reclamation project is taking place, despite protests from local citizens. We collected river water from the source to the reclamation area.

At the source of the river

Upper reaches of the river

At the source, the water creates an almost transparent crystal, and water from the upper reaches of the river revealed a breathtaking crystal.

Water flowing through the city

Water right before it reaches the bay

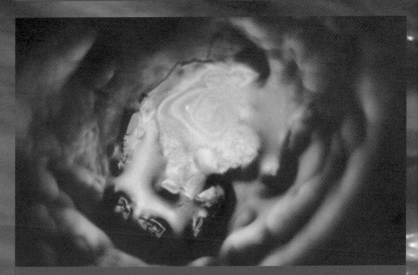

Pond in a planned land-reclamation area

As the water moves along, it becomes polluted until crystal formation becomes difficult or even impossible. At the land-reclamation site where the water has been diverted, the puddle water resulted in a tragic-looking crystal. When water is prevented from flowing, it dies.

Three faces shown by the river

The Fuji River flows through a plain at the foot of Mt. Fuji. We made crystals at the upper reaches, midstream, and lower reaches of the river.

Upstream (Metori Yusui springwater)

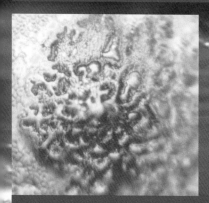

Midstream

Downstream

The springwater from the upper reaches creates a crystal that looks like a beautiful pearl. In the midstream, where the water runs through a rural area, a deformed crystal is formed. At the lower reaches of the river, the water becomes cleaner.

Japanese water collected at several locations

The difference in crystals formed from city water and water from springs, waterfalls, lakes, and rivers is profound.

Doryuonotaki Waterfall, Yamanashi prefecture

Towada Lake, Tohoku

Doryuonotaki Waterfall is close to the Fuji River. It resulted in a well-formed crystal. Water from Towada Lake in northern Japan has some degree of pollution, but the crystal was relatively well-balanced.

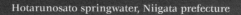

Hotarunosato springwater, Niigata prefecture

Sumida River, Tokyo

This crystal from Hotarunosato, which means "home to the firefly," created tiny light-like crystals, as might be expected. Sumida River, one of the main rivers in Tokyo, is now cleaner than it has been in years, but it is still not clean enough to form a crystal.

Crystals from water shown photographs of nature

We took pictures of crystals formed by water that had been shown photographs such as flowers and natural scenery.

A photograph of cherry blossoms

A photograph of a lotus flower

The water was shown a photograph of a fox in the lush forest under-growth. The resulting crystal is bright and sharp but perhaps a little melancholy also.

The photograph is of a tree silhouetted against a crescent moon at dusk. The unique crystal formed seems to mimic the shape of the tree.

The brilliant autumn leaves in the photograph created a crystal that appears to be formed by leaves before they have fallen from the trees.

This photograph of an ancient tree on Yakushima Island resulted in a large, unique crystal that seems to be teeming with life.

Crystals formed by water shown names of various religions

We exposed the water to the names of the world's five major religions.
What might you expect?

Buddhism

Buddhism was the only religion to result in a crystal with a hollow center.
Perhaps this indicates the pathway to the next life, per the Buddhist teachings of
reincarnation. It is a beautiful and well-balanced crystal.

Christianity

The tips of the crystal seem similar to Christmas trees. The fine detail and shape remind us of the religious ornaments of churches of the Middle Ages.

Judaism

The commandments of Judaism are said to be strict, but this crystal is certainly gorgeous and unconstrained. The overlapping layering of the crystal is also unique.

Islam

This also resulted in a beautiful crystal, perhaps indicative of the religion's comprehensive doctrine.

Hinduism

This crystal hexagon is almost perfectly geometrical, as if you were peering
into a kaleidoscope.

The power to heal is the power of life.
We tested Effective Microorganism (EM), a patented microorganism being promoted in Japan in various products, which has the ability to cleanse the environment, along with flower essence and aroma oil.

Water with EM added to it

EM is made from a microorganism good for the environment and health. Just a small amount diluted in water resulted in a crystal teeming with vitality.

Gorse flower

Scottish primrose

Cherry blossom

These are photographs of crystals made with the vibration of flowers. They all resemble beautiful, blossoming flowers. The finely detailed crystals seem to have a healing effect.

Iona pennywort

Valerian flower

Elderflower

All of these crystals are charmingly beautiful. Just looking at these pictures may make you feel your mind and body heal.

The vibration of aroma oil reflected in water

Chamomile

The vibration of aromatherapy oil was transferred to water using a device that transmits hado. The result is a crystal almost identical to the flower itself.

Fennel

This crystal is influenced by fennel flower essence. Like blossoms floating in the water, the crystal is a brilliant representation of the flower.

Love and Thanks in three languages

The crystals formed when water is exposed to Love and Thanks seem to express all that is beautiful in the world. We compared the results in English, German, and Japanese.

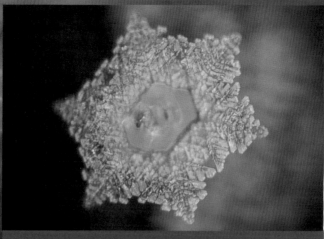

Love and Thanks (English)

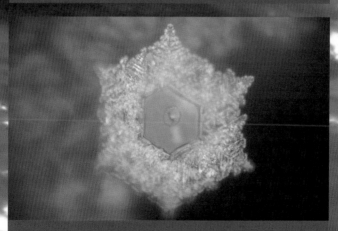

Love and Thanks (German)

The two crystals look almost identical. Maybe this indicates that love and thanks have the same vibration no matter what the language. These are words that can be understood by everyone in the world.

Love and Thanks (Japanese)

Everything begins and ends with love and thanks. Wouldn't it be wonderful to live each day with the beauty of this crystal within your heart?

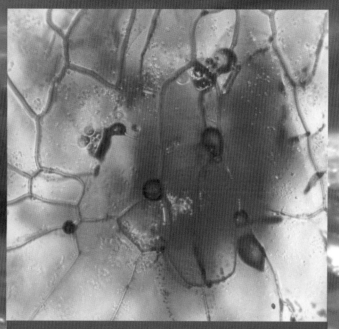

Rainwater from Tokorozawa in Japan, three years previous

Tokorozawa on the outskirts of Tokyo was known as a
dioxin-polluted waste dump.

Rainwater from Tokorozawa in Japan, present

Thanks to the efforts to clean and improve the area by the local citizens, the rainwater has changed, as evidenced in the most recent photo.

"With thanks to all our readers"

Further information on Masaru Emoto's
groundbreaking work, as well as
related materials, may be found at
Beyond Words Publishing Inc.
20827 N.W. Cornell Road, Suite 500
Hillsboro, OR 97124-9808
www.beyondword.com